Study of **Subject-Verb Agreement, Narration Change**, Use of **Punctuation;** including **Analysis, Synthesis** & **Split-up**

Study through charts, division, explanations and examples

Mr. Peter

Made with ❤ on the Notion Press Platform

www.notionpress.com

DEDICATION

Dedicated to my father, my first teacher, guide and philosopher

Writer's Academic works:

1. Study of Nouns, Pronouns, Adjectives & Articles (detail study) ISBN: 979-842-211-856-4 / 979-888-704-109-4
2. All about Verbs (Forms, Functions, Conjugation, Tense, Voice Change, Forming Questions & Negation) ISBN: 979-840-441-149-2 / 979-888-704-411-8
3. Study of Adverbs, Prepositions, Conjunctions & Interjections ISBN: 979-840-785-010-6 / 979-888-704-532-0
4. Detail Study of Phrases, Clauses & Sentences, including Idioms & Phrasal Verbs ISBN: 979-840-881-405-3 / 979-888-704-582-5
5. Study of Subject-Verb Agreement, Narration Change, Use of Punctuation; including Analysis, Synthesis & Split-up (Study through charts, division, explanation and examples) ISBN: 979-880-723-013-3 / 979-888-704-674-7
6. **Peter's 'English Grammar, A Complete Version of English Grammar,** (detail study, explanation & examples) ISBN: 979-879-725-020-3 / 979-888-704-463-7
7. **Question Bank of English Grammar & Composition (Learn through Exercises)** ISBN: 979-883-531-890-2 / 979-888-733-132-4
8. **Rhetoric & Prosody** (A handbook of Figures of Speech, rhymes, feet of poetic lines for High School Students) ISBN: 979-840-526-645-9 / 979-888-684-952-3
9. Picture Composition: For Primary Level, Std-I to V (Development of Writing Skill from Single Sentence Formation to Paragraph Writing, incl. question patterns and answer guide) ISBN: 979-888-805-249-5 (B&W) / 979-888-783-066-7 (color print)
10. Steps to Composition (Development of Writing Skill, Part-1), includes Picture Composition, Essay & Story Writing ISBN: 979-884-408-069-2 / 979-888-805-001-9
11. Development of Writing Skill, Part-2 (includes Letter Writing- Business Letters, Application for Jobs, Letters to Editor, bank authorities, Institutional Heads & others) ISBN: 979-835-689-886-0 / 979-888-833-455-3
12. Development of Writing Skill, Part-3 (includes- E-mails, Poster Making, Notices, Processing, Dialogue, Article, Speech & Debate Writing as well as Diary entry, Summary and Reporting) ISBN: 979-836-392-249-7 / 979-888-869-544-9
13. **A Book of Advanced Writing Skill, the Complete Version** (incl Part-1, 2 & 3) ISBN: 979-836-472-826-5 / 979-888-869-835-8

Author page URL's:
https://www.amazon.com/author/mr.peter
https://www.amazon.in/~/e/B09QW2P4TY *(For Indians, this and next)*
https://notionpress.com/store/s?NP_Books%5Bquery%5D=Mr.+Peter
https://www.amazon.co.uk/~/e/B09QW2P4TY
https://www.amazon.de/~/e/B09QW2P4TY
https://www.amazon.fr/~/e/B09QW2P4TY
https://www.amazon.co.jp/~/e/B09QW2P4TY
https://www.amazon.es/~/e/B09QW2P4TY
https://www.amazon.it/~/e/B09QW2P4TY
https://www.amazon.com.br/kindle-dbs/entity/author?asin=B09QW2P4TY

For Readers from India and nearby, you may place order with notionpress.com
Visit notionpress.com and type 'Mr. Peter' in the search box; give order of books to **avail elegant discounts** *using the following* **Coupon Codes;** as, unique00, bulk00, Deal1 and so on against the books: (if not work, contact to https://www.facebook.com/profile.php?id=100081822070172 or (5) Books Campaigns, Free Coupons, Learning English Grammar & Composition | Facebook

Coupon Codes	**Book Name**	**Buy for**	**Discount %**	**Rebate Prices**
unique00	**Advanced Writing Skill, the Complete Version** (incl. Part-1, 2 & 3)	1 copy	15	~~780~~ 663
PujaDeal10	Development of Writing Skill, Part-3	1 copy	18	~~365~~ 300
PujaDeal9	Development of Writing Skill, Part-2	1 copy	18	~~365~~ 300
PujaDeal8	Steps to Composition (Development of Writing Skill, Part-1)	1 copy	20	~~300~~ 240
PujaDeal7	**Rhetoric & Prosody (for High School**	1 copy	20	~~240~~ 192

Study of **Subject-Verb Agreement, Narration Change,** Use of **Punctuation;** including **Analysis, Synthesis & Split-up**

	Students)			
PujaDeal6	**Question Bank of English Grammar & Composition**	1 copy	20	~~559~~ 448
PujaDeal5	Study of Subject-Verb Agreement, Narration Change, Use of Punctuation; including Analysis, Synthesis & Split-up	1 copy	20	~~301~~ 241
PujaDeal4	Detail Study of Phrases, Clauses & Sentences, including Idioms & Phrasal Verbs	1 copy	20	~~290~~ 232
PujaDeal3	Study of Adverbs, Prepositions, Conjunctions & Interjections	1 copy	20	~~260~~ 208
PujaDeal2	All about Verbs (Forms, Functions, Conjugation, Tense, Voice Change, Forming Questions & Negation)	1 copy	18	~~420~~ 345
PujaDeal1	Study of Nouns, Pronouns, Adjectives & Articles (detail study)	1 copy	20	~~280~~ 224
unique01	**Peter's 'English Grammar'** (Complete Version of English Grammar)	1 copy	23	~~1201~~ 925
	FOR COPIES MORE THAN ONE			
bulk00	**Advanced Writing Skill, the Complete Version** (incl. Part-1, 2 & 3)	2 to 5000 copies	23	~~780~~ 601
Deal11	Development of Writing Skill, Part-3	2 to 5000 copies	24	~~365~~ 278
Deal10	Development of Writing Skill, Part-2	2 to 5000 copies	24	~~365~~ 278
Deal9	Steps to Composition (Development of Writing Skill, from Primary to Secondary Level)	2 to 5000 copies	26	~~300~~ 222
Deal8	**Rhetoric & Prosody**	2 to 5000 copies	26	~~240~~ 178
Deal7	**Question Bank of English Grammar & Composition**	2 to 5000 copies	28	~~559~~ 403
bulk01	**Peter's 'English Grammar'** (Complete Version of English Grammar)	2 to 5000 copies	30	~~1201~~ 841
Deal5	Study of Subject-Verb Agreement, Narration Change, Use of Punctuation; including Analysis, Synthesis & Split-up	2 to 5000 copies	26	~~301~~ 223
Deal4	Detail Study of Phrases, Clauses & Sentences, including Idioms & Phrasal Verbs	2 to 5000 copies	26	~~290~~ 215
Deal3	Study of Adverbs, Prepositions, Conjunctions & Interjections	2 to 5000 copies	26	~~260~~ 193
Deal2	All about Verbs (Forms, Functions, Conjugation, Tense, Voice Change, Forming Questions & Negation)	2 to 5000 copies	26	~~420~~ 311
Deal1	Study of Nouns, Pronouns, Adjectives & Articles (detail study)	2 to 5000 copies	26	~~280~~ 208

CONTENTS

Chapters	Pages
Outline Of the Book	viii
1. Sentence & Kinds of…	9
2. Analysis of Simple Sentence, as Subject & Predicate	11
3. Study 'Subject Adjuncts', & 'Extension to Predicate'	15
Subjects & Adjuncts to Subject variant	20
Extension or Adverbial Adjuncts	23
How an object shaped	26
Attributes or Adjuncts to Object	28
Complement (Subjective or Objective)	30
Infinitive & Gerundial Infinitive	34
4. Analysis of Compound & Complex Sentence	37
Analysis of a compound sentence	38
Analysis of a complex sentence	42
5. Synthesis, or Joining of Simple Sentences	46
To make Single Simple Sentence	47
To make a Compound Sentence	55
To make a Complex Sentence	58
6. Split-up of a Sentence	61
Split up through Analysis	65
Split up of Complex Compound	69
Split-up of 'Quoted Sentence', 'Parenthetic Phrase & Clause'	70
Use of 'It' & 'There' in Split-up	74
7. Direct & Indirect Speech (Change of Narration)	76
5 Major Rules of Narration Change	78
Narration Change: Assertive Sentence	82

Narration Change: Interrogative 83
Narration Change: Imperative 84
Use of Vocatives in Imperative: 88
Use of 'Let' in the Narration Change 89
Narration Change: Optative 90
Narration Change: Exclamatory 91
Reporting of 'One-word Replies' & 'Multiple Sentences' 94
8. The Conversion or Transformation of Sentences 95
Conversion of Adverb 'too' 96
Conversion of Degrees (adj. & adv.) 97
Conversion of Active & Passive 99
Conversion from Affirmative to Negative 101
Conversion of Interrogative to Assertive 103
Conversion of Exclamatory to Assertive 104
Conversion of Simple, Compound & Complex 108
Conversion of Narration 113
Conversion: From One to Thirty-Two 114
9. The Use of Punctuations (includes 16) 116
Use of Capital Letters 117
Brackets, Asterisk, Dot-dot-dot & Oblique 124
Parenthesis 125
10. Subject & Verb Agreement 127

Outline Of the Book

The book includes the chapters of --**how to analyze simple, compound and complex sentences**—to know different basic parts of a sentence (as subject, predicate, and their adjuncts or extension) for better understanding the formation of a sentence. It helps you to build, modify, change your sentence from one to another. If you learn to analyze a sentence properly, **synthesis or joining** is a very easy task for a student. Better repair comes with the knowledge of different parts of an engine. And **split-up** is it's another important part to nurture. The mood of Speech, the so-called **narration change** (from direct to indirect, and vice-versa) have been included with illustration of rules and examples. A prolonged exercise of transformation of sentences (**conversion**) from one to thirty-two has been included to give you taste and foster your knowledge how far you did gather till date. **Sixteen punctuations** with signs or symbols and their significance cum uses are shown with examples in sentences. And to the last, but not least, given importance to your need for a summary of **subject verb agreement** to enrich the knowledge to make you prepared for your exams. Thanking you, lots of regard from Mr. Peter.

1. Sentence & Kinds of...

1. **Sentence & Kinds of...**

A group of words with one or more finite verbs unit that makes a complete sense or expresses a complete thought, is called a Sentence; as,

1) What can we do to help you?
2) He is an aashiq.
3) We carved not a line, **and** we raised not a stone.
4) Our hoard is little, ***but*** our hearts are great.
5) I thought of Raghab who was at that moment was attending a party.
6) She gave me the same feeling (that) she contributed last.

In the above sentences, there are two—1 & 2, each has only one finite verb. There are three sentences—3, 4 & 6 which have two finite verb units each; and there is only one sentence, sentence no-5, has three finite verb units (helping and main verb together is called a unit of finite verb; and *a unit of finite verbs* denotes one clause or a simple sentence.)

And every sentence must begin with **a Capital Letter** & ends, either with a **Full Stop (.) or** a **Question (?) or** an **Exclamation Mark(!)**; as again in the following,

- You don't know what you are talking about!
- How many days will you take to say this?
- You are a good girl.

And, based on number of finite verbs or number of clauses, use of relative pronoun or adverb, co-ordinate or sub-ordinate conjunctions, a sentence may be a simple sentence, or a compound or complex.

For analysis a simple sentence is different from analysis a compound or complex.

And for analysis, it also needs the basic knowledge about a phrase, a clause, and about the formation or structure of a sentence, which we have already gathered or studied through the previous chapters or books. However, read the following sentences, and guess which are phrases, clauses or sentences.

2. **Read the Sentences:**
   - The sun rises ***in the east***.
   - Humpty Dumpty sat ***on a wall***.
   - There came a giant ***to my door***.
   - It was a sunset ***of great beauty***.
   - The tops ***of the mountains*** were covered with snow.
   - Show me ***how to do it***.

In the above, the bold and italic words—are merely examples of phrases, denoting— *direction, position, movement, quality, possession* and an action acted upon (object) or *manner of action.*

3. **Again, read the followings:**
   - He has a chain *which is made of gold*.
   - People *who pay their debts* are trusted.
   - We cannot start *while it is raining*.
   - I think (that) *you have made a history*.

   - People *who pay their debts* are trusted.
   - We cannot start *while it is raining*.
   - I think (*that) you have made a history*.

- The above underlined are the examples of clauses, which are formed of a group of words with one unit of finite verb (i.e., the unit of finite verb may be formed of single verb or in the combination of a main and helping verbs together), and each sentence is an example of complex sentence. a compound too is made of two or more clauses.
  - The followings are the examples of compound sentences, the clauses in them are joined by co-ordinate conjunctions:

- We carved not a line, **and** we raised not a stone.
- She must weep, **or** she will die.
- **Either** he is mad, **or** he feigns madness.
- We can travel by land **or** water.
- They toil not, **neither** do they spin.
- Our hoard is little, ***but*** our hearts are great.
- Something certainly fell in; ***for*** I heard a splash.

If face difficulty to understand or identify the above; as a phrase, clause or sentence (as the simple, compound or complex), you are suggested to revise the chapters of phrase, clause & classification of sentences (based on structure), before go to next 'about the analysis of sentence' (simple, compound and complex). Best of luck.

2. Analysis of Simple Sentence, as Subject & Predicate

4. **Read the Sentences:**
   - The flower bloomed.
   - Bob painted.
   - The girls of the team were all good students.
   - Bill told everyone about the wreck.
   - Mary sobbed.
   - Tom plays the piano well.

5. **Subject & Predicate:** Every complete sentence has two main parts: a subject and a predicate.

Simply, 'subject' is the **doer of an action, who or what does something**; or the person or a thing **of whom or which something is said;** as,

- *The flower* bloomed.
- *Bob* painted.
- *The girls of the team* were all good students.
- *Bill* told everyone about the wreck.
- *Mary* sobbed.
- *Tom* plays the piano well.

Basically, the **term *'predicate' refers to the finite verb or the unit***. However, in broad sense, it includes the entire part of the verb along with its object or objects, adverbials and complement in the sentence. Though, briefly to say, **'what is said about the subject', is called predicate**; as,

- The flower *bloomed*.
- Bob *painted*.
- The girls of the team *were all good students*.

- Bill *told everyone about the wreck.*
- Mary *sobbed.*
- Tom *plays the piano well.*

6. Simple Subject & Complete Subject:

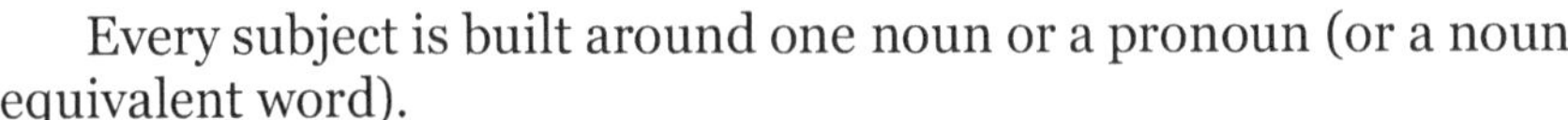

Every subject is built around one noun or a pronoun (or a noun equivalent word).

The ***simple subject*** *(what we told as* ***'root subject'*** *in the heading)* is only the *main word* in a complete subject about whom or what something is said; as the following:

- The four new **students** arrived early.

✓ In the sentence, the underlined is the complete subject, while the word in bold, is the Simple or Root Subject. So, the simple subject in the sentence is- **students.**

The **complete subject** is the main noun word or noun equivalent word along with its all qualifiers or adjuncts (adjective or adjective equivalent words, are popularly known as adjuncts to a subject). In the above sentence, the underlined is an example of complete subject.

7. Simple Predicate & Complete Predicate:

A **simple predicate** (or the root predicate word) is always the verb or verbs (that link up with the subject) that expresses an action or state about the person or thing; as,

- Sara's sister ***took*** *us bowling yesterday*.
- The four new students ***arrived*** *early*.

✓ Here, in the above, while the underlined are the examples of Complete Predicate, the simple or root predicates are only the unit of finite verbs. Thus, the Root or Simple predicate words are respectively— **'took'** & **'arrived'**, written in bold in the lines.

The **Complete Predicate** is the verb and all its modifiers (adverb or adverbials), objects & complement, which are popularly known as the **extension to predicate**.

In the above sentences, the underlined, which are respectively —

'took us bowling yesterday' & **'arrived early'**—are the examples of **Complete Predicates**.

8. **Practice, find out 'simple subject' & 'complete subject' from the followings:**
    - **I** am a teacher.
    - **Arindam Dutta** is a doctor.
    - **Chetan** is a student of class X.
    - **'Chetan'** reads in class X?
    - **Burza Khalifa** is a large building.

➢ Who is a teacher? Who is a doctor? Who is a student? Who reads in class X? Which is a large building? (Always, ask question to the verb. About who or what are the sentences? —are the simple or complete subject in the sentences.)

9. **More examples, try yourself:**
    - She lifted the cake to take it to Raghav.
    - That is the real reason.
    - I don't need anyone.
    - I thought you might be hungry.
    - My phone rang.
    - Old friends are old friends.
    - Bob, Peter & Shyam visit there.
    - You are crazy.
    - What are you doing here?
    - Please, don't pressurize me.

10. **Now, find out 'simple predicate' & 'complete predicate' from the same sentences, taken earlier:**
    - I **am** *a teacher*.
    - Arindam Dutta **is** *a doctor*.
    - Chetan **is** *a student of class X*.
    - 'Chetan' **reads** *in class X*.
    - Burza Khalifa **is** *a large building*.

- What's telling about 'I' in the first sentence?
- What's telling about 'Arindam Dutta' in the 2nd sentence?

- What's telling about 'Chetan' in 3rd & 4th sentences?
- What is told of Burza Khalifa?

✓ When the underlined words are examples of **complete predicates**; the words, written in bold—are the examples of **simple predicates.**

✓ Thus, the simple predicate words are— **'am' 'is', is, reads, & 'is'** respectively.

11. **Ways to find out 'predicate'?**
    - Ask question to the subjects; as, "what is he" or "what are they doing" / what does he or it do? etc.?
        - ✓ 'He ***is a doctor***. (What is he?)
        - ✓ He ***is running***. (What is he doing?)
        - ✓ She ***is studying***, etc. (What is she doing?)

12. **Let's check, read the followings and find out *subject* & *complete subject*, *predicate* & *complete predicate* from them:**

    a. Rony and his dog run on the beach every morning.
    → About whom is the sentence?
    → Who run on the beach every morning?

    b. We spilled popcorn on the floor.
    → About whom is the sentence?
    → Who spilled popcorn on the floor?

    c. My little brother broke his finger.
    → About whom is the sentence?
    → Who broke his finger?

    d. His Uncle Bob asked for directions.
    → About whom is the sentence?
    → Who asked for directions?

    e. Those soldiers carried guns.
    → About whom is the sentence?
    → Who carried guns?

    f. Our honorable guests arrived in time.
    → About whom is the sentence?
    → Who arrived in time?

✓ ***Your answer, in each case, is the 'subject' of the respective sentence.***

Now find out 'predicate & 'complete predicate from them:

→ What's telling about 'him' or 'them' in the sentences?

→ What do they do? / What are they doing? Or what are they in their profession? /What is stating about a thing? /What do they have or possess or be?

- ***Here, your answer, in each case, is the 'predicate' of the sentence respectively, simple & complete.***

13. **Compound Subject:** A Compound Subject is made up of 'more than one noun or pronoun'; as,
    - ***Team pennants***, ***rock posters*** and ***family photographs*** covered the boy's bedroom walls.
    - ***Her uncle*** and ***she*** walked slowly through the art gallery and admired the beautiful pictures exhibited there.
    - ***My little brother*** and ***my cousin*** broke their fingers.
    - ***His Uncle Bob*** and ***Aunt Betty*** asked for directions.
    - ***Those soldiers*** and ***agents*** carried guns.

14. **Compound Predicate:** A Compound Predicate is made up of more than one verb relating to the same subject in the sentence.
    - Mother ***mopped*** and ***scrubbed*** the kitchen floor.

    - My little brother ***bruised*** and ***broke*** his finger.
    - His Uncle Bob ***looked*** and ***asked for*** directions.
    - Those soldiers c***arried*** and ***used*** guns.

3. Study 'Subject Adjuncts', & 'Extension to Predicate'

15. In the first stage of analysis of a sentence, we have studied, a sentence has two main parts— **the Subject** & **the Predicate**; as,

SUBJECT	PREDICATE (Chart-1)
1) Dogs	bark.
2) The sun	gives light.
3) The child	is dead.
4) The boys	made Rama captain.
5) My father	gave me a watch.
6) The flames	spread everywhere.
7) The flames	spread in every direction.
8) The hour to prepare lessons	has arrived.

Each Sentence has a **Subject** & a **Predicate** (they are essential to a sentence).

We may also call these **two main parts** of a Simple Sentence as *'subject-group'* & *'predicate-group'*, or 'complete subject' & 'complete predicate'; and they consist of:

Subject Group	Predicate Group
1. Simple subject or root subject-word, and 2. Adjuncts to the subject, if any (the qualifiers or attributes),	1. The unit of finite verb cum simple predicate, 2. Object (Direct & Indirect), 3. Attributes to the object (qualifiers), 4. Complement, (subjective & objective), 5. Adverb or adverbials, which are also known as Adverbial Qualification or Extension to the Predicate.

16. **Simple & Complete Subject:** The main noun or noun equivalent word with its qualifiers that denotes a person or thing who or which does anything, or about whom or which something is said.

The point is, a **subject may consist of one word** or **more words**.

Read the sentences: -

1) **Dogs** /bark.
2) **India** /is our motherland.
3) The **sun** /gives light.
4) The **child**/ is dead.
5) The **boys** / made Rama captain.
6) My **father**/ gave me a watch.
7) The **flames**/ spread everywhere.

8) The **flames**/ spread in every direction.
9) **Swimming** in the pond / is now not a good habit.
10) The **hour** to prepare lessons/ has arrived.

- In sentence-1 & 2, the subject consists of one word, i.e., 'dogs' & 'India' respectively.
- In the sentences from 3 to 8, the subjects consist of two words;
- In sentence 9, it consists of four words; while
- In sentence -10, the subject consists of five words only.

In case of subjects that consist of several words, there is always one word which is most important than the others. The chief word in the complete subject is known as **Root** or **Main Subject-word**' or the so-called **Simple Subject**'. Thus, the **bold word** in each is the example of **simple subject** in the sentences, while the underlined are the examples of Complete subjects.

❑ **A complete subject consists of** *simple subject word along with its modifiers* **or** *the adjuncts*.

The adjuncts to the subject may vary from adjective to participle, possessive noun or pronoun to case in apposition, and the most common thing is an article. Now, read them in details.

- '*Little child* wants to play.'
- *Stone walls do* not make a prison.
- A barking sound *the shepherd* hears.

→ The main subject words are **'child'**, **'walls'**, & **'shepherd', which are also called simple subjects**, when 'little' is an adjective; 'stone' is a noun used as adjective to form the compound noun 'stone walls', and 'the' before shepherd is an article.

17. **Simple & Complete Predicate:** It denotes the unit of finite verb (main with helping) along with its objects, complement and adverbials.

A word or a group of words that **is said about the subject** (said about the person or thing).

Like a complete subject, **a complete predicate too may consist of one or more words;** as,

1. Peter / **runs**.
2. Peter / **runs** fast.
3. Peter / **runs** very fast.

4. India / **is** our motherland.
5. My father/ **gave** me a watch.
6. The boys / **made** Rama captain.
7. The flames/ **spread** everywhere.
8. Swimming in the pond / **is** now not a good habit.

- In sentence 1, the Predicate consists of one word. In sentences 2 & 7, the predicate consists of two words; while,
- In sentences 3 to 6, the complete predicate consists of three words, and
- In sentence 8, the complete predicate consists of six words. Thus, **a predicate may consist of any number.**

The most essential word in a Predicate is always the finite verb (i.e., the unit of finite verb, the main with its helping) **which is termed as 'simple predicate'; then comes others.**

If the Predicate consists of one word, that is definitely the finite verb. If that consist of several words, the chief or essential word of all others is also the finite verb. Thus, the most important word in the predicate is always the **finite verb**. So why, the verb is also called the **Main Predicate Word**'.

Thus, in sentences from 1 to 8, the bold words are the example of **main predicate words**, and the underlined are the example of complete predicate.

A complete predicate includes simple predicate, object to the verb, adjuncts or attributes to object, complements (subjective or objective) and adverbials (which is popularly known as **Extension to Predicate**).

18. Exercise-1: In the following sentences separate **the Subject** & **the Predicate Group** & then underline the **main subject word** & the **predicate-word**:
    1. The cackling of geese saved Rome.
    2. All matter I indestructible.
    3. No man can serve two masters.
    4. A sick room should be well aired.
    5. I shot arrow in the air.
    6. Up went the balloon.
    7. The naked everyday he clads.
    8. Into the street the piper stepped.
    9. Sweet are the uses of adversity.
    10. Dear, gentle, patient, noble Nell was dead.

Check your Answer:

If we separate the **Subject** & the **Predicate Group** & then underline the **main subject word** & **predicate-word in the following way**:

Subject Group/complete subject	Predicate Group/ complete predicate
1. The **cackling** of geese	1. **saved** Rome.
2. All **matter**	2. **is** indestructible.
3. No **man**	3. can **serve** two masters.
4. A sick **room**	4. should be well **aired**.
5. **I**	5. **shot** arrow in the air.
6. The **balloon**.	6. **went** Up.
7. The naked **he**	7. **Clads** every day.
8. the **piper**	8. **Stepped** into the street.
9. the **uses** of adversity.	9. **are** Sweet.
10. Dear, gentle, patient, noble **Nell**	10. **Was** dead.

19. **What shaped the Subject**
(Generally a Noun or a Noun Equivalent word)

The ***main Subject Word***, or Simple Subject is always a Noun or a Pronoun, or a Noun Equivalent word. However, it is often used with its qualifiers, we say ***'adjuncts' to the subjects***, form **'complete subject'**.

A 'Noun Equivalent' is a word or words other than Nouns or Pronouns that does the work of a Noun in the sentence, that may be *an adjective*, *a gerund*, *participle*, *infinitive verb* or a *phrase* & even *a clause*; as,

1. ***He*** / tried his best.
2. The ***rich*** / are not always happy.
3. ***Talking*** overmuch / is the sign of vanity.
4. ***To err*** / is human.
5. ***To find fault*** / is easy.
6. ***That you loved her*** / was known to all.

The bold italic words are the simple subjects in the above sentences.

Note: *Sometimes, the main or simple subject can't form expected meaning with a single word and we need more words to make it more* *expressive and meaningful as a subject is called* ***the complete subject****, i.e., in sentences 3 to 6.*

How is a Subject Shaped (by noun or noun equivalent along with its attributes or adjuncts):

Subjects & Adjuncts to Subject variant

1. A Noun: 2. A Pronoun: 3. An Adjective: 4. An Infinitive: 5. An Infinitive Phrase: 6. A Gerund: 7. A Verbal Noun: 8. A Phrase: 9. A Clause: 10. A Quotation:	1. **India** is our motherland. 2. **He** reads a story. 3. **The virtuous** are happy. 4. **To error** is human. 5. **To have done that** is risky. 6. **Swimming** is a good exercise. 7. The writing of letters is now a lost art. 8. **Success at any cost** was his aim. 9. That you stand first is known. 10. **"All the world is a stage"** occurs in Shakespeare.

20. **Adjuncts to the subject** (so called Enlargement or Attributes)— are mainly the Adjectives or Qualifiers. They are known as **Enlargement** or **Attribute to the Subject,** we already read some examples. Read here some more examples:
    1. ***New*** brooms / sweep clean.
    2. ***Barking*** dogs / seldom bite.
    3. ***Peter's*** father / was a teacher.
    4. ***My*** views / are same as hers.
    5. Akbar, ***the emperor***, / invaded Kashmir.
    6. An Akbar, ***my friend***, is an Insurance Agent of Balurghat.
    7. ***A*** desire ***to excel*** / is commendable.
    8. ***A*** stitch ***in time*** / saves nine.

The bold italic words are the attributes or adjuncts to the subjects in the above sentences, whereas the underlined are the complete subjects in the sentences.

The attributes or adjuncts may vary from one to other. They may be **Adjective**, **Participle**, **Possessive Noun** or **Pronoun, Noun in apposition**, **Gerundial Infinitive**, even **Adverbials** that do work like an adjective in the sentences.

Study the Sentences (chart-2)

Sent No	Subject			Predicate
	Subject word	**Attribute**	**Type of attribute**	
1	brooms	New	Adjective	sweep clean.
2	dog	Barking	Participle	seldom bite.
3	father	Peter's	Possessive Noun	is a teacher.
4	views	My	Possessive Adjective	are same as hers.
5	Akbar	the emperor	Noun in Apposition	invaded Kashmir.
	Akbar	my friend	Noun in Apposition	is an Insurance Agent of Balurghat.
6	desire	A, to excel	Article & Gerundial Infinitive	is commendable.
7	stitch	A, in time	Article; Adverbial but do the work of an adjective	saves nine.

Study the Adjuncts to subject-variants

1. An adjective: 2. A Participle: 3. A Participial Phrase: 4. Noun/Gerund, used as Adjective: 5. A Gerundial Infinitive: 6. A Noun or Pronoun in Possessive case: 7. A Noun or an Emphatic Pronoun in apposition:	1. A good boy is loved by all. 2. Flying clouds are seen in the sky. 3. The boy playing on the lawn is my brother. 4. The street boy is laughing. Drinking water should be pure. 5. Water to drink should be pure. 6. My brother is ill. / His father's watch is stolen. 7. Rama, my brother, is ill. He himself did it. 8. A man of principle is liked by all.

8. A Preposition with an Object: 9. An Adv. Used as an Adj. 10. An Adj. Clause:	9. The then king did it. The down train is coming. 10. Boys *who work hard* succeed.

21. Exercise-2

In the following sentences, **pick out the complete subjects, then separate simple subjects from their Attributes**:

1. The boy, anxious to learn, worked hard.
2. A burnt cow dreads the fire.
3. Birds of feather flock together.
4. The attempt to scale the fort was an utter failure.
5. The days of our youth are the days of our glory.
6. Ill habits gather by unseen degrees.
7. The dog, seizing the man by the collar, dragged him out.
8. The streets of some of our cities are noted for their crookedness.
9. A house divided against it cannot stand.
10. Deceived by his friends, he lost all hope.
11. The man carrying a hoe is a gardener.
12. One man's meat is another man's poison.
13. My days among the dead are past.
14. With his white hair un-bonneted, the stout old sheriff comes.

Study the Analysis of the sentences in chart-3:

Sent. No	Subject			Predicate
	Subject word	**Attribute**	**Type of attribute**	
1	boy,	The, anxious to learn,	Article, Adjective with object	worked hard.
2	cow	A burnt	Article with Participle	dreads the fire.
3	Birds	of feather	Preposition with Noun as qualifying words or Adj. Equiv.	flock together.
4	attempt	The, to scale the fort	Article, Gerundial Infinitive	was an utter failure.

5	days	The, of our youth	Article, prepositional phrase denoting time.	are the days of our glory.
6	habits	Ill	Adjective	gather by unseen degrees.
7	dog,	The, seizing the man by the collar,	Article; qualifying words or adj. equivalent	dragged him out.
8	streets	The, of some of our cities	Article, words show part of something	are noted for their crookedness.
9	house	A, divided against itself	Article, adj. phrase	cannot stand.
10	he	Deceived by his friends,	Adj. phrase	lost all hope.
11	man	The, carrying a hoe	Article, Noun in Apposition	is a gardener.
12	meat	One man's	Adj. with noun's possession	is another man's poison.
13	days	My, among the dead	Possessive adj., Noun with preposition as qualifying words	are past.
14	sheriff	With his white hair un-bonneted, the stout old	Both adj. equivalent	comes.

Extension or Adverbial Adjuncts

22. If we divide a complete predicate, we have

Helping verb+ the predicate word + object + complement + adverbials

The adverb, adverb-equivalent or adverbials is sometimes called as **Extension** or **Adverbial Qualification**.

A complete predicate, often, includes a complement. The complement may be Subjective or Objective (if the verb is Intransitive, the complement is Subjective, if the Verb is Transitive, the complement is always Objective. Study in details).

Study the following sentences in the next chart, and try understand their parts or components.

1. He went home.
2. He rose to go.
3. The flames spread in every direction.
4. Spring advancing, the swallows appear.

Sl. No	Subject			Predicate		
	Subject-word	***Attribute***	***Type of attribute***	***Predicate word/Verb***	***Adverbial Qualification***	***Type of Extension***
1	He			went	home.	Noun used as Adverb
2	He			rose	to go.	Infinitive used as adverb
3	flames	The	article	spread	in every direction.	Adv. phrase
4	swallows	The	article	appear	Spring advancing.	Absolute phrase, denoting time.

23. **Adverbial Adjuncts to Predicate:** The adverb or adverb equivalent words are also known as Predicate Modifiers, Extension or Adverbial Qualification. Read the chart:

1. An Adverb:	1. He acted **wisely**.
2. Adj. used as an Adv.	2. He died **happy**. (happily)
3. An Adverbial Phrase:	3. They walk **side by side**. (How?)
4. A Participle:	4. He went away **disappointed** (or weeping.)
5. A Gerundial Infinitive:	5. He came **to see me**. (Why?)
6. An Adverbial Object:	6. He walked **all day/five miles**. (How long? / How far?)
7. A Preposition with Object:	7. He arrived **in time**. (When?)

8. An Absolute Phrase: 9. An Adverbial Clause	8. **The sun having set**, we left the place. (Referring time) 9. He went away **after I had left**.

24. Transitive Verbs & Objects (Direct & Indirect)

If the verb is transitive, it must have at least one object, and the single object must be Direct Object, either it is animate or inanimate object, [like having Principal & helping verb. If a sentence has single verb, that must be the principal verb, if two, another may be helping verb. For, a compound or complex sentence must have two or more principal verbs in them] A Transitive Verb may have two or more objects. If have two, one is Direct, and another is Indirect. [Generally, the inanimate object is the Direct and the animate Object is the Indirect Object, though that may differ]. Read the examples:

1) Birds builds nest.
2) I know him.
3) Peter gave Rakesha pencil.
4) Naughty children love fighting.
5) The foolish crow tried to sing.
6) Our soldiers tried to scale the cliff.
7) All good children pity the poor.
8) I promised him a present.
9) He teaches us Geometry.
10) Father bought Minia doll.

The Analysis of the above Sentences:

Sl. No	Subject		Predicate		
	Subject-word	**Attribute**	**Verb**	**Object**	**Types of Objects**
1	Birds		builds	nest.	the Object is a Noun
2	I		know	him.	A Pronoun
3	Peter		gave	Rakesh a pencil.	Indirect & Direct Object

4	children	Naughty	love	fighting.	A gerund or verbal Noun
5	crow	The foolish	tried	to sing.	An infinitive
6	soldiers	Our	tried	to scale the cliff.	'to scale'— an infinitive; 'the cliff'—the object of infinitive verb
7	children	All good	pity	the poor.	An Adjective used as a Noun
8	I		promised	him (i.o.)	a present. (d.o.)
9	He		teaches	us (i.o.)	geometry. (d.o.)
10	Father		bought	Mini (I.O.)	a doll (d.o.)

How an object shaped

25. **Study, 'how is an Object shaped?'**

1. A Noun: 2. A Pronoun: 3. An Adjective: 4. An Infinitive: 5. A Gerund: 6. A Phrase: 7. A Clause: 8. A Quotation:	1. I like the **boy**. 2. We did **it**. 3. Everybody loves the **good**. 4. He likes **to swim**. 5. He likes **swimming**. 6. I know **how to do it**. 7. I know **that he did it**. 8. He said, **"Do it at once."**

To identify objects properly in the analysis of a sentence, we need to know of them (here briefly; for details go to the chapter of 'Glossary of Objects' & 'Transitive Verbs'.

Study the Objects glossary: including 2 mains

Objects	***About them & Examples***

Direct Object	The thing or person an action is directly acted upon is called Direct Object. If there are two objects, generally, the inanimate thing tends to be the Direct Object. (However, it may differ.) If there is only one object in the sentence, it is always the Direct Object, irrespective of animal or thing. • I gave him ***a book***.
Indirect Object	An action for whom or to who, or to what is acted, is called the Indirect Object. When there are two objects, the object that refers to man or animal tends to be an Indirect Object. (However, it may also differ.) • I gave ***him*** a book.
Factitive object	When an object of Transitive Verb requires a complement, the verb is called Factitive, and its object is termed as Factitive Object. **A Factitive Object always requires a complement.** • I made ***him*** a fool. (F. O. + complement) • We made ***him*** captain. **'fool'** & **'captain'**—are complements in the sentences.
Cognate object	In case of intransitive verbs **when an object generates from the verb itself.** ('cognate' means originates 'what is similar in meaning') • He runs ***a race***. • She sings ***a song***.
Retained object	It means the object which is left or retained in Passive voice. We learnt a verb may have two or more objects in a sentence. If there are both Direct & Indirect objects, either one takes the place of the subject in Passive, whereas another is retained or left as it was; the left one or retained one object is termed accordingly its meaning. • A book was given **me** by my father. • I was given **a book** by my father.
Reflexive Object	When an object reflects the pronoun in the subject, is called the reflexive object. Read the examples. • They hurt ***themselves.*** • I taught ***myself.***
Infinitive Object	When an infinitive verb forms an object of a verb. • He likes ***to go***. • She loves ***to sing***.
Object of an	When an infinitive verb takes an object itself; as, • He likes to go ***to school.*** • She loves to sing ***Rabindra Sangeet***.

Infinitive Verb	

26. The Points *to be Noted*:

- **If a sentence has only one object** (i.e., if a finite verb has only one object) **that must be the Direct Object** (irrespective of animate or inanimate).
- *Considering this*, all the above-mentioned objects as, Infinitive Objects (to go, to sing), Reflexive Objects (myself, themselves), Cognate Objects (a race, a song), Factitive Object (him)—are also the **Direct Objects** in the sentences.
- In case of the Retained object, either Direct or Indirect object may take the place of a subject, and the other is retained. So, a retained object may be a direct or an indirect.
- **Read again**, if there is one, that must be the Direct object, irrespective of animate or inanimate; but, if there are two, Direct object be termed with the most important one, upon whom or which the action is acted upon directly; as,

1. He shot his gun to the castle. (Targeting the castle).
   - Here, 'gun' is Direct Object, 'castle'—is the Indirect.

2. The police shot him to death. (here 'him' is the direct object. The action is directly acted upon him.)

3. He hit him with a stick.
   - Here again, 'him' is the Direct Object, while 'a stick' is an Indirect.

4. Teacher gave us some tasks to do at home.
   - And here, 'tasks' is Direct Object, while 'us' is the Indirect Object.

- So, we need must consider the importance of the word, not based upon animate or inanimate to be Direct or Indirect Object in the sentence.

Attributes or Adjuncts to Object

27. **Attributes** or **Adjuncts to the Object:** As some words, like adjectives, participles or articles—adds meaning or qualifies the noun or pronouns in the subjects, so as they do also to the objects. **Like subjects**, objects may have the same kinds of **adjuncts or attributes to qualify or add meaning to them**.

Read the followings sentences, and study the adjuncts to the objects:

1. He shot *a big* **panther**.
2. The world knows **nothing** *more of its greatest men*.
3. The Eskimos make **houses** *of snow & ice*.
4. *Her* **arms** across her breast she laid. (She laid her arms across her breast.)
5. The architect drew *a* **plan** for the house.
6. Serpents cast *their* **skin** once a year.
7. Rock *the* **baby** to sleep.
8. He enjoys *his master's* **confidence**.
9. I recognize *his* **voice** at once.
10. Cut *your* **coat** according to your cloth.

In the above sentences, the bold words are the examples of **Objects**, when the underlined and italic words are their **adjuncts** or **attributes**.

Study the following charts of Analysis showing the attributes of Objects:

Sl. No	Subject		Predicate			
	Subject-word	**Attribute**	**Verb**	**Object**	**Object attribute / Complement**	**Adverbial Qualification Or others**
1	He		shot	panther.	*a big*	
2	world	The	knows	nothing	*of its greatest men.*	*more*

3	Eskim os	The	make	houses	*of snow & ice.*	
4	she		laid.	arms	*Her*	across her breast
5	archite ct	The	drew	plan	*a*	for the house.
6	Serpe nts		cast	skin	*their*	once a year.
7			Rock	baby	*the*	to sleep
8	He		enjoys	confide nce.	*his master's*	
9	I		recogn ize	voice	*his*	at once.
1 0			Cut	coat	*your*	according to your cloth

Complement (Subjective or Objective)

28. A complement is **a word** or **a phrase** or **a clausal structure** that completes the meaning of a **noun or noun equivalent that are used either as a subject or an object**. Thus, complements are subjective or objective.
In case of Intransitive (or Linking) verb, when verbs require more words other than the simple predicate and adverbials, the words are termed as subjective complement which generally complete the sense of the subject; as,

He is a student.

(Here, student is a complement to the intransitive verb. And as it refers back to the subject, it is called subjective complement.)

A complement itself is usually a noun or an adjective, <u>a verb form like to be</u> a or a participle or a gerund, an infinitive verb, or an adverb, <u>used as an adjective</u> or a <u>clausal structure like</u> –ing clause **or** 'wh' clause.

<u>Study the chart:</u>

29. **Study the following sentences, and identify complements after separate the complete predicates.**

1. Black clouds <u>are gathering</u>. The sky <u>grew **dark**</u>.
2. The boys <u>have been reading</u>. They <u>are dancing</u>.
3. She <u>spoke distinctly</u>. The boy <u>ran a mile</u>. He <u>is **worried**</u>.
4. He <u>is a **student**</u>. I <u>was a **teacher**</u>. He <u>**is professional**</u>.
5. Venus <u>is a **planet**</u>. It <u>is **me**</u>. The workman <u>seems **tired**</u>.
6. The book <u>is there.</u> The house <u>is **to let**</u>. Shyamali is <u>**he, not she**</u>.
7. The building <u>is **in a dilapidated condition**</u>. John <u>became a **soldier**</u>.
8. Roses <u>smell **sweet**.</u> The child <u>appears **pleased**.</u>

The Underlines are the complete Predicates, whereas the words in bold are Complements to the Subject. The complements are generally a noun, or pronoun, an Adjective, infinite or others. (Study in details in the respective chapter of verb & complement.)

30. Exercise-3

Underline the complete Predicate first & then pick out the complement in each of the following sentences, and say whether it is a Noun, an Adjective, or others.:

1) The earth is round. He looks happy. Sugar taste sweet.
2) The old woman is dead. The weather is cold. The child is there.
3) He became unconscious. He is a good type of the modern athlete.
4) The old gentle man is of a gentle disposition.
5) The children look healthy. To-day she seems sad.
6) The cup is full to the brim. His grammar is hocking.
7) Ugly rumors are about him and his girl-friend.
8) Peter and his quarrelsome spouse were never a pride of their village, and there were more two such couples.
9) This morning he seems in a good spirit. Giving to the poor is lending to the Lord.
10) The matter appears of considerable importance. Every man is the architect of his own fortune.

31. **Transitive Verbs of Incomplete Predication & Objective Complement:**

We said, a transitive verb has object or objects. But, sometimes, Transitive verb too requires a complement. In spite have its object the verb cannot complete its sense. It requires then extra words beside the object. The extra word or words are known as Complement. As it actually completes the sense of the object, the complement is known as **Objective Complement**. Read the examples:

1) The boys made Rama Captain.
2) The jury found him guilty.
3) His parents named him Peter.
4) He kept us waiting.
5) Nothing will make him repent.
6) His words filled them with terror.
7) Shyam called his cousin a genius.
8) Exercise has made his muscles strong.
9) He kept us in suspense.
10) The court appointed him the guardian of the orphan child.

Study the following chart relating Object & Objective Complement:

Sl. No	Subject		Predicate		
	Subject-word	***Attribute***	***Verb***	***Object***	***Complement***
1	boys	The	made	Rama	Captain.
2	jury	The	found	him	guilty.
3	parents	His	named	him	Peter.
4	He		kept us		waiting.
5	Nothing		will make	him	repent.
6	words	His	filled	them	with terror.
7	Shyam		called	his cousin	a genius.
8	Exercise		has made	his muscles	strong.
9	He		kept us		in suspense.
10	court	The	appointed	him	The guardian of the orphan child.

32. **Adjuncts to Subject or Object & Adv. Adjuncts:** Adverbial adjuncts are often confounded with complements. It is well to remember that words, phrases or clauses which show — ***how, when, why*** or ***where*** an action is performed, are adverbial adjuncts. The adverbial adjuncts directly modify the verbs, whereas, the complements are related to Subjects or Objects in the sentences. However, here we will compare **the adjuncts to subjects** and **the adverbial adjuncts** in the sentences. Read the chart:

As adjuncts to subject	*As adverbial adjuncts to predicate*
1. The **defeated** team also got a cup. (adj. equivalent) 2. The **crying** woman arrived there.	1. She went away **laughing**. (adv. equivalent) 2. I saw a tiger **roaring**.

3. The **bereaved** mother came to Lord Buddha. 4. The **laughing** girls are students.	3. The woman **disappeared** weeping. 4. The cow is seen **wounded**.

Infinitive & Gerundial Infinitive

33. Know the use of **'gerundial infinitive'**. When an infinitive is used with a Noun or a Pronoun to form subject or object is called **'gerundial infinitive'**.

A Gerundial Infinitive can be used both in the subject & in the predicate group. Study the chart, how do they form & work:

In subject group	*In predicate group*
❑ **Examination to pass** is not so hard. (adj. equivalent) o Noun with infinitive verb ❑ **Women to consider** mother was a great teaching of Lord Ramakrishna. ❑ **To love her** was a good experience.	❑ He went to market **to buy medicine**. (adv. equivalent) o Noun with infinitive verb ❑ His teachings were **to develop inner possibilities.** ❑ My friend came **to see me.**

See the difference between: **Infinitive** & **Gerundial Infinitive**

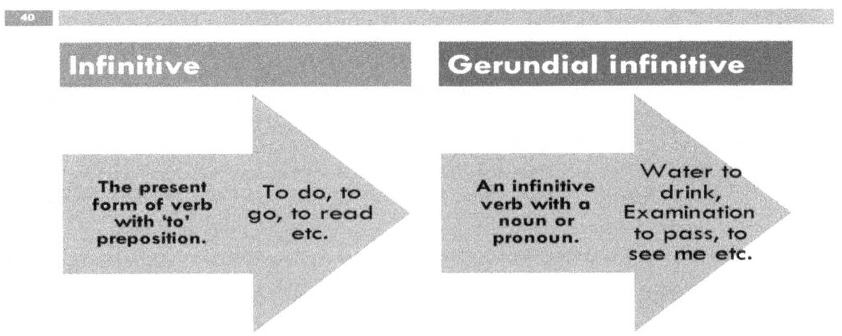

34. A Preposition generally precedes before a Noun or a Pronoun, as discussed and we learnt in the chapter of Preposition. The noun after a preposition is sometimes known as the 'object of a preposition.' Here we will see through chart how a **Preposition is used with a Noun** both in subject & object group.

In Subject	In Predicate
1. A man **of principle** is respected by all. 2. Arriving in time is our habit. 3. A girl **in the garden** is seen watering plants by all. 4. Dry leaves **falling from trees,** is a natural sight. 5. The book **on the table** is mine.	1. All respect a man **of principle**. 2. We arrived **in time**. 3. I saw a girl **in the garden** watering the plants 4. The dry leaves fall ***from* the trees.** 5. I place my book ***on* the table**
➢ In subject they are adjective equivalent: mostly a preposition with noun acts as a relative or adj. phrase.	➢ In predicate they, besides being an adjective equivalent, sometimes also **do function of an adverbial**, modifying a verb, or an adjective or another adverb; as in sentences 2 to 5.

35. The role of a Part of Speech may alternatively be changed according to uses and needs. Study the alternative use of adverb & adjective:

Use of adv. as adj. in sub. group	**Use of adj. as adv.** in pred. group
1. The **fast train** derailed this morning. 2. **The then** Prime Minister had signed the treaty.	1. He breathed **ice/dead**. 2. She sang **happy**.

36. Drawing Conclusion to the **<u>Analysis of a Simple Sentence.</u>** Read the Sentences and analyze them into Subject & Predicate Group and show their adjuncts or adverbial qualification:

1. Dushshashan, quite pale with fright, rushed from the battle field.
2. Determination to do one's duty is laudable.
3. Around the fire, one wintry night, the farmer's rosy children sat.

4. Home they brought the warrior dead.
5. His friends elected him secretary of the club.
6. This circumstance certainly makes the matter very serious.
7. My uncle has been teaching me mathematics.
8. Who are you?

Study the Analysis of the (Simple) Sentences

Sl. No	Subject		Predicate			
	Subject-word	**Attribute**	**Verb**	**Object**	**Complement**	**Adverbial Qualification**
1	Dushshashan	quite pale with fright	rushed			from the battlefield
2	Determination	to do one's duty	is		laudable	
3	children	the farmer', rosy	sat			Around the fire, one wintry nigh,
4	they		brought	the warrior	dead	Home
5	friends	His	elected	him	secretary of the club.	
6	circumstances	This	makes	the matter	very serious	certainly
7	uncle	My	has been teaching	mathematics, me		
8	you		are		Who	

Read some more examples:

1. The other day my younger brother saw two men fighting each other.

2. The Judge, accepting the verdict of the jury, found the prisoner tremendously guilty.
3. On hearing of my misfortune, all my friends ran to my help.
4. An intelligent boy, the son of a very poor man, badly needs your help to be able to continue his studies.

Study another phase of Analysis of Simple Sentences

Adjunct to Subject	Subject Proper	Finit e Verb	Object with Adjectives	Complem ent	Adverbial Adjunct
my younger	brother	saw	two men	fighting with each other	The other day
The, accepting the verdict of the jury	Judge	found	the prisoner	guilty	tremendo usly
all my, On hearing my misfortune	friends	ran	----	----	to my help
An, Intelligent, the son of a very poor man	boy	needs	your help	to be able to continue his studies	badly

4. Analysis of Compound & Complex Sentence

37. The Analysis of a Sentence (Compound & Complex) refers to the 'breakdown the sentence (compound or complex) primarily into – Principal, Co-ordinate & Sub-ordinate Clauses, and then, if necessary, to breakdown each clause further as Subject and

Predicate and according to their adjuncts or extensions (as we have done with a Simple Sentence in the previous chapter).

Analysis of a compound sentence

38. **Read the Sentences:**
1. All good children pity the poor, and poor the poorest.
2. Naughty children love fighting, do you?
3. Our soldiers tried to scale the cliff and they did succeed.
4. He came to see me when I was in trouble; but when I asked him for pecuniary help, he pleaded inability.
5. On my return from school, I went to my mother to ask for food; but I found that she was lying ill of fever and my younger sister was nursing her.

39. **In analyzing a Compound Sentence,**

a) First, break up the sentence into as many clauses as there are units of Finite Verbs, expressed or understood (each unit finite verb takes the main and helping verbs together);

b) Identify Principal & Co-ordinate Clauses;

c) Identify any Sub-Ordinate Clause, if any there is, and show their relation with the Principal or the Co-ordinate;

d) Next, analyze each clause separately, if necessary or asked by your teacher; otherwise, for exams, generally, mere clause analysis is enough for a compound or complex sentences.

You may check the analysis of the above five sentences in the following way, as given in the chart. Study thoroughly:

	a)	b)	c)	d)
	Principal Clause	Sub-ordinate with Principal	**Co-ordinate Clause**	Sub-ordinate with Co-ordinate
1.	All good children pity the poor,		and poor the poorest.	
2.	Naughty children love fighting,		(and) do you?	

3.	Our soldiers tried to scale the cliff		and they did succeed.	
4.	He came to see me	when I was in trouble;	But... he pleaded inability.	when I asked him for pecuniary help,
5.	On my return from school, I went to my mother to ask for food;		i) but I found ... ii) and my younger sister was nursing her.	that she was lying ill of fever

40. **Read again for more examples:**

1. Though I was ill, I tried my best; but, as ill luck would have it, all my exertion ended in smoke.
2. Long ago, when I was yet a student, I once went to Darjeeling, where I was charmed by the beautiful mountain scenery that greeted me on all sides.

If we analyze the sentences accordingly the above, follow the chart:

	a)	b)	c)	d)
	Principal Clause	Sub-ordinate with Principal	Co-ordinate Clause	Sub-ordinate with Co-ordinate
1.	I tried my best;	Though I was ill,	but, all my exertion ended in smoke.	as ill luck would have it,
2.	Long ago, I once went to Darjeeling,	when I was yet a student,	Where (and there) I was charmed by the beautiful mountain scenery	that greeted me on all sides.

As per clauses, the above two sentences have been analyzed. Now, if we want further analysis of the above clauses as **subject**, **predicate**, **adjuncts to subjects** and **extension to the predicate**, then, we should follow the next step (what we have done with simple sentences).

Sl. No	Clauses	Kind of Clause		Subject		Predicate			
			Connective	Subject Proper	Adjuncts to Subject	Predicate Verb	Object with adjuncts	Complement	Adv. Adjuncts
1-a)	I tried my best	Principal		I		tried	my best.		
b)	Though I was ill	Adv Clause	though	I		was		ill.	
c)	but... all my exertion ended in smoke	Co-ordinate	but	exertion	all my	ended			in smoke.
d)	as ill luck have it	Adv Clause	as	luck	ill	have	it		
2-a)	Long ago, I once went to Darjeeling	Principal		I		went			Long ago, once, To Darjeeling
b)	When I was yet a student	Adv Clause	when	I		Was		A student	yet

c)	Where I was charmed by the beautiful mountain scenery	Co-ordinate	Where (=and there)	I		Was charmed	By the ... scenery		
d)	that greeted me on all sides.	Adjective Clause	that (understood)	that (=the scenery)		greeted	me		On all sides.

41. Exercise-1

Analyze the following compound sentences:

1. I am sorry that you have disobeyed my orders; however, as this is my first offence, I let you off this time with a simple warning, and hope you will not give me any trouble in future.
2. We should all love India, where we were born and which is one of oldest countries in the world, and should never do anything that may bring discredit upon her in any way.
3. Just as the destruction was completed Newton opened the chamber door, and perceived that the labors of twenty years were reduced to a heap of ashes.
4. I was in the same school with the person you speak of; but as he was senior to me by a few years we did not mix much with each other.

To do so, use the following table, or make such ones, after the first step:

Complete Analysis of a Compound

9

Sl. No	Clauses	Kind of Clause		Subject		Predicate			
			Connective	Subject Proper	Adjuncts to Subject	Predicate Verb	Object with adjuncts	Complement	Adv. Adjuncts
1									
2									
3									
4									
5									

Analysis of a complex sentence

42. In analyzing a Complex Sentence, we have to do almost same thing, we did for a Compound.

First, to divide a complex sentence into clauses, based on number of the unit of Finite Verbs. Identify their types, as Principal, Sub-ordinate or Co-ordinate clauses. If need further analysis, have to follow the next step what is done with a simple sentence.

Study the sentences:

1. When I was a student, I was one day taken to task by the Principal of my college for having played on behalf of an outside club, though he had ordered us not to do so.
2. Having been informed that my brother who had gone to Delhi to attend the Legislative Assembly was lying seriously ill of fever there, I applied for one week's leave of absence in order that I might go to him to arrange for proper treatment.

Study the analysis **(the first step is to divide sentences into clauses):**

Clauses	Kind of Clause	Connectives
(a) I was one day...of an outside club (b) When I was a student (c) though he ...not to do so	Principal clause Sub. Adv. Clause, qualifying '**was taken** in (a)' Sub. Adv. Clause, qualifying '**having played** in (a)'	when though
2. (a) Having been **informed**, I **<u>applied for</u>** one week's leave of absence (b) That **my brother** was lying seriously ill of fever there (c) Who had gone to Delhi to attend the Legislative Assembly (d) In order that I might go to him to arrange for proper treatment.	Principal clause Sub- Noun Clause, object to verb '**informed**' in (a)' in participle form Sub. Adj. Clause, describing '**my brother**' in (b)' Sub. Adv. Clause, describing '**applied for**' in (a)'	that who In order that

Now further analysis of the above clauses as '**subject**', '**predicate**', '**adjuncts to subject**' and '**extension to the predicate**' (The 2nd step of analysis).

Adjunct to Subject	Subject Proper	Finite Verb	Object with Adj.	Complement	Adverbial Adjunct
	I	was taken	by the Principal of my college	to task	one day, for having played on behalf of an outside club,
	I	was		a student	when
	He	had ordered	us		not to do so
Having been informed	I	applied			for one week's leave of absence

my	Brother	was lying	seriously ill of fever there
	who	had gone	to Delhi to attend the L. Assembly
	I	might go	to him to arrange for proper treatment.

43. A Few Difficulties in Analysis

1. In case "Quoted sentences": -

- **He said**, "I cannot come to you today. My brother is ill and I have to attend on him. You may, however, expect me tomorrow."

→ **The quotation consists of three sentences**, which cannot be taken separately in their relation to the principal verb '**said**', three sentences together act as the **object** to the verb, **'said'**.

→ The quotation has been taken in this case **as a long compound word**, a **noun equivalent**, and object to some transitive verb. Here, it is 'said'; as, — I said, "**I am ill**". What did I say? = that I am ill = an object to the verb 'said'.

→ I was surprised by his '**I don't care**' attitude (a **compound adjective** describing the noun 'attitude')

→ However, if we treat each sentence separately, analysis is same, as we did of earlier simple sentences.

2. 'Parenthetic' expressions or phrases:

1) He is, **I am sure**, something of a poet.
2) His conduct, **I believe**, is good.
3) Why do you, my friend, **I don't know**, hate me?
4) Why do you, **it is not clear**, not talk to me now-a-days?
5) But you should, **I am likely agreed**, do so.

→ All the above are simple sentences while the **bold written words are parenthetic expressions**; almost like the 'Phrase or Noun in apposition'.

→ As phrase in apposition, the parenthetic expressions **are thrown into the sentence, to provide more information to the**

main and they easily can be taken out without injuring the sense of the main.

→ 'Parenthetic expressions or Phrases' can be analyzed separately, as an independent sentence.

❑ **'Parenthetic'** expressions in compound

1) He is, **I am sure**, something of a poet & his poetry are too good to read by others.
2) His conduct, **I believe**, is good & too good to converse with.
3) Why do you, my friend, **I don't know**, give me light and snatch it away?
4) Why do you, it **is not clear**, begin to talk and stop forever?

→ All the above are compound sentences with two principals while the **bold written words are parenthetic expressions**; and they can be analyzed separately, as told already. In the sentences they **are thrown to provide more information to the main sentence, subject or verb**; and they may be taken out without injuring the sense of the main.

❑ **'Parenthetic'** expressions in complex

1) He is, **I am sure**, something of a poet who reads alone his poetry.
2) His conduct, **I believe**, is what is not suitable for his own age.
3) He is the man who, **I believe**, did it.
4) This is the boy who, **I think**, came the other day.

→ All the above are complex sentences with only one principal & one sub-ordinate clauses while the **bold written words are parenthetic expressions**; and they can be analyzed separately as independent sentence.

→ **Like Parenthetic Expressions, t**here are also the '**Parenthetic Phrases**'.

❑ Some more Parenthetic Phrases

1) He is, **to tell the truth**, not quite frank.
2) I was, **to be frank**, much surprised.
3) I am, **of me**, ok.

→ In above all cases, the '**phrases within commas before & after'**, can be analyzed separately and similarly can be taken out without injuring the main sense.

3. In case introductory- 'There' & 'It'

1) **There** is a man here. (A man is here/Here is a man.)
2) **There** was once a king in India, named Dasaratha.
= (Once a king, named Dasaratha lived in India.)

→ 'There' in the above cases have lost its force of meaning as an adverb of place, and are used only to introduce the sentence.
→ As custom '**There**' will fall in the group as an **Adv. adjunct** but it is better to treat it as '**Introductory Subject**' as– '**It** is raining.'

44. Exercise-2, **Analyze the following Complex Sentences:**

1) I know that he was absent at that time.
2) There is no knowing when he will come.
3) Tell me where she lives.
4) Had I been present there, sure I opposed this.
5) It is a misfortune that you could not do anything.
6) You can never expect that, because you are talented, others will willingly make way for you in order that you may go ahead of them.
7) As I was absent at the time the incident took place, I had to depend for information about it on my friend who had seen everything with his own eyes from his house that stood close by.
8) The two men, who were following a few yards behind me, came to a halt when they saw me stop.

5. Synthesis, or Joining of Simple Sentences

45. Literally, **'Synthesis'** is nearly the opposite term of **'Analysis', and yet to be different;** whereas, it is *nearest the opposite* of the word **'split-up'.**

The term **'Synthesis'** means 'Joining of Simple Sentences' to make a larger Simple Sentence, or a Compound or Complex Sentence; So, we will discuss this chapter under three main heads:

A. Synthesis of Simple Sentences to make a Simple Sentence (other than they were),
B. Synthesis of Simple Sentences to make a Compound Sentence,
C. Synthesis of Simple Sentences to make a Complex Sentence.

On the other hand, **'Split-up'** means to break up a sentence to make as far possible independent sentences (**not like:** what actually 'Analysis' does). In split-up, we try to give independent form of the essential or important parts of a sentence to make as far possible smaller independent simple sentences. Read more about it in the next chapter.

A. Synthesis of Simple Sentences to make a Simple Sentence (other than they were),

The following are the chief ways of combining two or more Simple sentences into one or single Simple Sentence:

a) By using a Participle,
b) By using an Infinitive,
c) By using a Preposition with a Noun or Gerund,
d) By using a Noun or a Phrase in Apposition,
e) By using the Nominative Absolute Construction,
f) By using an Adverb or Adverbial Phrase.

To make Single Simple Sentence

a) By using a Participle:
- He jumped up. He ran away.
  = *Jumping up*, he ran away.
- He was tired of play. He sat down to rest.
  = *Tired* (or, *being tired*) of play, he sat down to rest.

b) By using an Infinitive:
- I have some duties. I must perform them.

= I have some duties *to perform*.

- He wanted to educate his son. He sent him to Nalanda.
  = He sent his son to Nalanda *to educate* him.
- He is very fat. He cannot run. =He is too fat *to run*.

c) By using a Preposition with a Noun or a Gerund:

- He has failed many times. He still hopes to succeed.
  = *In spite of failures* many times he hopes to succeed.
- Her husband died. She heard the news. She fainted.
  = *On hearing* the news of her husband's death, she fainted.

d) By using a Noun or Phrase in Apposition:

- Mr. Pranab Mukherjee was elected the President of India. He was the Finance Minister of India before that.
  = Mr. Pranab Mukherjee, *the former Finance Minister of India*, was elected the President of India.
- Geoffrey Chaucer was born in 1340. He is the first great English Poet.
  = Geoffrey Chaucer, *the first great English poet*, was born in 1340.

e) By using the Nominative Absolute Construction:

- The soldiers arrived. The mob dispersed.
  = *The soldiers having arrived*, the mob dispersed.
- The town was enclosed by a strong wall. The enemy was unable to capture it.
  = *The town having been enclosed by a strong wall*; the enemy was unable to capture it.

f) By using an Adverb or Adverbial Phrase:

- The sun set. The boy had not finished the game.
  = The boys had not finished the game *by sunset*.
- The Moon rose. The journey was not ended.
  = The Moon rose *before the end of the journey*.

Now, read in details

46. Joining by use of a **Participle**: (for more practice) (1)

1. The magician took pity on the mouse. He turned it into a cat.
   = ***Taking** pity on the mouse*, the magician turned it into a cat.

2. We started early. We arrived at noon.
   = ***Starting*** *early*, we arrived at noon.
3. We met a man. He was carrying a log of wood.
   = We met *a man* ***carrying*** a log of wood.
4. He seized his stick. He rushed to the door.
   = ***Seizing*** *his stick*, he rushed to the door.
5. The hunter took up his gun. He went out to shoot the lion.
   = ***Taking*** *up his gun*, the hunter went out to shoot the lion.
6. A crow stole a piece of cheese. She flew to her nest to enjoy the tasty meal.
   = ***Stealing*** *a piece of cheese*, the female crow flew to her nest to enjoy the tasty meal.
7. The wolf wished to pick a quarrel with the lamb. He said, "How dare you make the water muddy?"
   = ***Wishing*** *to pick a quarrel with the lamb*, the wolf said, "How dare you make the water muddy?"
8. A passenger alighted from the train. He fell over a bag on the platform.
   = ***Alighting*** *from the train*, the passenger fell over a bag on the platform.
9. Nanak met his brother in the street. He asked him where he was going.
   = ***Meeting*** *his brother in the street*, Nanak asked him where he was going?
10. My sistcr was charmed with the silk. She bought ten yards.
   = ***Being charmed*** *with the silk*, my sister bought ten yards.
11. The steamer was delayed by a storm. She came into port a day late.
   = ***Being delayed*** *by a storm* the steamer came into port a day late.
12. He had resolved on a certain course. He acted with vigor.
   = ***Having resolved*** *on a certain course*, he acted with vigor.
13. He staggered back. He sank to the ground.
   = ***Staggering*** *back*, he sank to the ground.
14. They had no fodder. They could give the cow nothing to eat.
   = ***Having*** *no fodder*, they could give the cow nothing to eat.
15. A hungry fox saw some bunches of grapes. They were hanging from a vine.

= A hungry fox saw some bunches of *grapes* ***hanging*** from a vine.

16. Cinderella hurried away with much haste. She dropped one of her little glass slippers.

= ***Hurrying*** *away with much hasty*, Cinderella dropped one of her little glass slippers.

47. Joining by use of an **Infinitive** (for practice) (2)

1) Napoleon was one of the greatest of Generals. He is universally acknowledged so.
   = Napoleon is universally acknowledged ***to be*** one of the greatest Generals.
2) He did not have even a rupee with him. He could not buy a loaf of bread.
   = He did not have even a rupee with him ***to buy*** a loaf of bread.
3) Every cricket team has a captain. He directs the other players.
   = Every cricket team has a captain ***to direct*** the other players.
4) You must part with your purse. On this condition only you can save your life.
   = You must part with your purse ***to save*** your life.
5) He went to Amritsar. He wanted to visit the Golden Temple.
   = He went to Amritsar ***to visit*** the Golden Temple.
6) The robber took out a knife. He intended to frighten the old man.
   = The robber took out a knife ***to frighten*** the old man.
7) He wants to earn his livelihood. He works hard for that reason.
   = He works hard ***to earn*** his livelihood.
8) The strikers held a meeting. They wished to discuss the terms of the employers.
   = The strikers held a meeting ***to discuss*** the terms of the employers.
9) He has five children. He must provide for them.
   = He has five children ***to provide*** for them.
10) I speak the truth. I am not afraid of it.
   = I am not afraid ***to speak*** the truth.
11) The old man has now little energy left. He cannot take his morning constitutional exercises.
   = The old man has now little energy left even ***to take*** his morning constitutional exercises.
12) The Rajah allowed no cows to be slaughtered in his territory. It was his custom.
   = It was the Rajah's custom not ***to allow*** cows to be slaughtered in his territory.

13) He formed a resolution. It was to the effect that he would not speculate any more.
= He formed a resolution to the effect ***not to speculate*** any more.

14) Everyone should do his duty. India expects this of every man.
= India expects every man ***to do*** his duty.

15) She visits the poor. She is anxious to relieve them of their sufferings.
= She visits the poor ***to relieve*** them of their sufferings.

16) He collects old stamps even at great expense. This is his hobby.
= This is his hobby ***to collect*** old stamps even at great expense.

17) He must apologize for his misconduct. It is the only way to escape punishment.
= He must apologize for his misconduct ***to escape*** punishment.

18) I have no aptitude for business. I must speak it out frankly.
= ***To speak it out frankly***, I have no aptitude for business.

19) He was desirous of impressing his host. So, he was on his best behavior in his presence.
= He was on his best behavior in the presence of his host ***to impress*** him.

20) He has risen to eminence from poverty and obscurity. It is highly creditable.
= It is highly creditable of him ***to rise*** to eminence from poverty and obscurity.

48. Synthesis by use of '**Prepositions with Nouns** or **Gerunds**' (for more Practice) (3)

1) He was ill during the last term. He was unable to attend the school.
= ***Due to ill*** during the last term, he was unable to attend the school.

2) I forgave her faults. That has not prevented her from repeating it.
= ***In spite of forgiving*** her faults that has not prevented her from repeating it.

3) The word of command will be given. You will then fire.
= You will fire ***on having*** the word of command.

4) He set traps every night. He cleared his house of rats.
= ***By setting*** traps every night, he cleared his house of rats.

5) The judge gave his decision. The court listened silently.
= ***On silence*** of the court, the judge gave his decision.

6) He has a good record. It is impossible to suspect such a man.

= ***Due to good record***, it is impossible to suspect such a man.

7) You helped me. Otherwise, I should have been drowned.
   = ***On having*** your help, I am saved from drowning.
8) I have examined the statement. I find many errors in them.
   = ***On examining*** the statement, I find many errors in them.
9) It rained hard. The streets were flooded.
   = ***On raining*** hard, the streets were flooded.
10) He amused us very much. He sang a funny song.
   = ***By singing*** a funny song, he amused us very much.

49. Synthesis by use of '**Nouns** or **Phrase in Apposition**' (for more practice) (4)

1) There goes my brother. He is called Rama.
   = There goes my brother, ***Rama***.
2) The cow provides milk. Milk is a valuable food.
   = The cow provides milk, ***a valuable food***.
3) Coal is a very important mineral. It is hard, bright, black & brittle.
   = Coal, ***a hard, bright, black & brittle substance***, is a very important mineral.
4) We saw the picture. It is a very fine piece of work.
   = We saw the picture, ***a very fine piece of work***.
5) Tagore's one of the most famous works is Gitanjali. Gitanjali is a collection of short poems.
   = Tagore's one of the most famous works is Gitanjali, ***a collection of short poems.***
6) Nicky's mom was a millionaire. She sent him to Australia for his higher education.
   = Nicky's mom, ***a millionaire***, sent him to Australia for his higher education.
7) Bagha was my faithful dog. After his death I never took another as my pet.
   = After death of my Bagha, ***a faithful dog***, I never took another as my pet.
8) Jawaharlal Nehru died in 1964. He was the first Prime Minister of India.
   = Jawaharlal Nehru, ***the first Prime Minister of India***, died in 1964.
9) He is selected as our captain. He is the first boy of our class.
   = He, ***the first boy of our class***, is selected as our captain.
10) His only son died before him. He was a lad of great promise.
   = His only son, ***a lad of great promise***, died before him.

50. Synthesis by use of 'Nominative Absolute Phrase' (for practice) (5):

When subjects are different, Nominative Absolute is popularly used for the Synthesis; as,

1) His friend arrived. He was very pleased.
   = *His friend having arrived*; he was very pleased. (**On arrival of his friend**, he was very pleased: **By Preposition with a Noun)**
2) The rain fell. The crops revived.
   = *The rain having fallen*, the crops revived.
3) The storm ceased. The sun came out.
   = *The storm having ceased*; the sun came out.
4) The holidays are at an end. Boys are returning to school.
   = *The holidays being at an end*, boys are returning to school.
5) It was a very hot day. I could not do my work satisfactorily.
   = *The day being very hot*, I could not do my work satisfactorily.
6) The king died. His fitting son came to the throne.
   = *The king having dead*, his fitting son came to the throne.
7) His father was dead. He had to support his widowed mother.
   = *Father being dead*, the son had to support his widowed mother.
8) Rain was plentiful this year. Rice is cheap everywhere.
   = *Rain being plentiful this year*, rice is cheap everywhere.
9) The prisoner was questioned. No witness came forward. The judge dismissed the case.
   = *The prisoner being questioned and no witness came forward*, the judge dismissed the case.
10) The letter was badly written. I had great difficulty in making out its contents.
   = *The letter being badly written*, I had great difficulty in making out its contents.
11) The sun rose. The fog cleared away. The light house was less than a mile away.
   = *The sun having risen*, the fog cleared away to see the light house less than a mile away.
12) The train was ready to leave the station. The passengers had taken their seats.
   = *The passengers having taken their seats*; the train was ready to leave.
13) The porter opened the gate. We entered.
   = *The gate being opened by the porter*, we entered.
14) The stable door was open. The horse was stolen.
   = *The stable door being open*, the horse was stolen.

51. Synthesis by use of an Adverb or Adverbial Phrase (6):

1) He answered me. His answer was correct.
   = He answered me *correctly*.
2) He forgot his umbrella. That was careless.
   = He forgot his umbrella *carelessly*.
3) The man is dead. It is certain.
   = *Certainly*, the man is dead.
4) The train is very late. That was usual.
   = *Usually*, the train is very late.
5) I shall come back. I shall not be long.
   = I shall come back *for a short duration*.
6) He kicked the goal-keeper. It was his intension to do so.
   = He kicked the goal-keeper *intentionally*.
7) She was obstinate. She refused to listen to any advice.
   = She *obstinately* refused to listen any advice.
8) He spent his all money. This was foolish.
   = He *foolishly* spent his all money.
9) He appealed for leave. It was not granted.
   = *Vainly* he appealed for leave.
10) It must be done. The cost does not count.
    = It must be done *at any cost*. (Adverb of Manner; also, can say: Preposition with a Noun)

52. **Exercise-1:** Combine the following set of sentences into Single Simple Sentences (Miscellaneous):

a) He was a leader. He did not follow other men. Such was his nature.
b) I bought this hat two years ago. It is still good. It is fit to wear.
c) He devoted himself to public affairs. He never took a holiday. This continued for thirty years.
d) The man was innocent. He could defend himself. He refused to speak. He was afraid of convincing his friend.
e) He stuck his foot against a stone. He fell to the ground. He made his clothes very dirty.
f) He goes to school. She wishes to learn. He wants to grow up honest, healthy and clever.
g) There was a man hiding in my garden. He was armed with a gun. He was a Pathan. My notice was drawn to it.
h) The soldiers were starving. Their ammunition was expended. Their clothes were in rags. Their leaders were dead. The enemy easily defeated them.

Check your Answer, Exercise-1:

Combine the following set of sentences into Single Simple Sentences (Miscellaneous):

- He was a leader. He did not follow other men. Such was his nature.

a) Being a leader, not to follow other men, was his nature.
- I bought this hat two years ago. It is still good. It is fit to wear.

b) This hat, bought two years ago, is still good and fit to wear.
- He devoted himself to public affairs. He never took a holiday. This continued for thirty years.

c) Devoting himself to public affairs, he never took a holiday for thirty years.
- The man was innocent. He could defend himself. He refused to speak. He was afraid of convincing his friend.

d) Being afraid of convincing his friend and yet having ability to defend himself, the innocent he refused to speak.
- He stuck his foot against a stone. He fell to the ground. He made his clothes very dirty.

e) Sticking his foot against a stone, he fell to the ground, making his clothes dirty.
- He goes to school. She wishes to learn. He wants to grow up honest, healthy and clever.

f) In order to learn, grow up honest, healthy and clever he goes to school.
- There was a man hiding in my garden. He was armed with a gun. He was a Pathan. My notice was drawn to it.

g) My notice was drawn to an armed Pathan hiding in my garden.
- The soldiers were starving. Their ammunition was expended. Their clothes were in rags. Their leaders were dead. The enemy easily defeated them.

h) Being starved, ammunition expended, clothes in rug & leaderless, easily they were defeated by the enemy.

To make a Compound Sentence

B. Synthesis of Simple Sentences (two or more) to make a Compound Sentence:

Simple Sentences may be combined to form a Compound Sentence by the use of **Co-ordinate Conjunctions**. There are four kinds of Co-ordinate Conjunctions; all can be used to form Compound Sentences; as,

A) *Joining by **Cumulative Conjunctions***, when the sentences express ideas of equal rank. Such conjunctions are— and, also, too, as well as, both—and, not only—but also, etc.

1) We carved not a line, **and** we raised not a stone.
2) God made the country **and** man, made the town.
3) Vishal & Virat are good bowlers. (Vishal is a good bowler & Virat is a good bowler.)

B) *Joining by **Adversative Conjunctions***, when expressing ideas contrast each other. Such conjunctions are — still, yet, only, but, however, nevertheless, though—yet, etc.

4) Our hoard is little, ***but*** our hearts are great.
5) The man is poor, ***but*** honest. (The man is poor, but he is honest.)
6) He is slow, ***but*** he is sure. I was annoyed, ***still*** I kept quiet.
7) I would come; ***only*** that I am engaged. He was all right; ***only*** he was fatigued.

C) *Joining by **Alternative Conjunctions***, when two or more sentences express alternation or selection between two or more. The conjunctions are— either...or, neither...nor, whether, or, etc.:

8) She must weep, **or** she will die. **Either** he is mad, **or** he feigns madness.
9) Is that story true **or** false? **Neither** a borrower, **nor** a lender be.
10) We can travel by land **or** water. They toil not, **neither** do they spin.
11) **Either** you are mistaken, **or** I am. Walk quickly, **else** you will not overtake him.

D) *Joining by **Illative Conjunctions***, for the sentences which express inference, or conclusion type ideas. The conjunctions are— therefore, for, so, then, so then, etc.:

12) Something certainly fell in; ***for*** I heard a splash.
13) All precautions must have been neglected, ***for*** the plague spread rapidly.

53. More Examples of Compound Sentences. Hope, you understand which simple sentences there are:

1) The moon was bright ***and*** we could see our way.
2) Night came on ***and*** rain fell heavily ***and*** we got very wet.
3) I shall do it now ***or*** I shall not do it at all.
4) He gave them no money ***nor*** he did he help them anyway.
5) He threw the stone ***but*** it missed the target.
6) He ***neither*** obtains success ***nor*** deserves it.
7) He is ***either*** mad ***or*** he has become a criminal.
8) He helped me, ***which*** (=and this/it) was very kind of him.

9) I went to Kolkata, ***where*** (=<u>and there</u>) I stayed for one month.
10) I went to the Principal, ***who*** (=<u>and he</u>) spoke kindly to me.

54. Combine each set of Simple Sentences to make a Single Compound Sentence:
1) He does well. He is nervous at the start.
2) The way was long. The wind was cold.
3) It is raining heavily. I will take an umbrella with me.
4) It was stormy night. We ventured out.
5) I am in the right. You are in the wrong.
6) We can travel by land. We can travel by water.
7) The train was wrecked. No one was hurt.
8) The paper is good. The binding is very bad.
9) The river is deep and swift. I am afraid to dive into it.
10) Bruce was lying on his bed. He looked up to the roof. He saw a spider.
11) Most of the rebels were slain. A few escaped. They hid in the woods and marshes. The rebellion was quickly suppressed.
12) Make haste. You will be late. There is no other train till midnight. That train is a slow one.

You may tally your answers with the following: (don't worry, variation may happen)

- He does well. He is nervous at the start.

1) He is nervous at the start, but he does well. (In spite of being nervous at the start, he does well.: **Simple Sentence**)

- The way was long. The wind was cold.

2) The way was long and the wind was cold.

- It is raining heavily. I will take an umbrella with me.

3) It is raining heavily, so I will take an umbrella with me.

- It was stormy night. We ventured out.

4) It was a stormy night, yet we ventured out.

- I am in the right. You are in the wrong.

5) I am in the right, but you are in the wrong.

- We can travel by land. We can travel by water.

6) We can travel by land and by water.

- The train was wrecked. No one was hurt.

7) Though the train was wrecked, yet no one hurt. /The train was wrecked, still no one was hurt.

- The paper is good. The binding is very bad.

8) Though the paper is good, its binding is very bad.

- The river is deep and swift. I am afraid to dive into it.

9) The river is deep and swift; therefore, I am afraid to dive into it.
   - Bruce was lying on his bed. He looked up to the roof. He saw a spider.

10) Lying on his bed Bruce looked to the roof and he saw a spider.
   - Most of the rebels were slain. A few escaped. They hid in the woods and marshes. The rebellion was quickly suppressed.

11) Killing most of the rebels, though few escaped hiding in the woods and marshes, the rebellion was quickly suppressed.
   - Make haste. You will be late. There is no other train till midnight. That train is a slow one.

12) Make haste, or you will be late, and the next train is not before till midnight and it is a slow one.

To make a Complex Sentence

C. Synthesis of Simple Sentences to make a Complex Sentence.

55. For joining two or more sentences to make single Complex, we generally do turn one or more simple sentences into Sub-ordinate Clause or Clauses (i.e., into **Noun Clause**, **Relative Clause** or to **an Adverbial Clause**), while the other is turned into the **Principal Clause**. For this goal, we need also to study or take a revision of Relative Pronouns, or Adverbs as well as go through the Sub-ordinate Conjunctions which are used to form Sub-ordinate Clauses. Study the examples carefully and see how the conjunctions (sub-ordinate), relative pronouns or adverb do join the sentences.

(1) Joining of simple sentences by turning one into a Noun Clause: In the following examples the Sub-ordinate Clause is a Noun Clause:

1) He will be late. That is certain.
   → = It is certain that he will be late.
2) She is drunk. That aggravates her offence.
   → = That she is drunk aggravates her offence.
3) He may be innocent. I do not know.
   → = I do not know whether he is innocent.
4) He is short-sighted. Otherwise, he is fit for the post.
   → = Except that he is short-sighted he is fit for the post.
5) The clouds would disperse. That was our hope. Our hope was cheering.
   → = Our hope that the clouds would disperse, was cheering.
6) The game was lost. It was the consequences of his carelessness.

→ = The consequence of his carelessness was that the game was lost.

(2) Joining by turning one simple sentence into Adjective or Relative Clause: In the following examples the Sub-ordinate Clause is made a Relative or Adjective Clause:

7) A fox once met a lion. The fox had never seen a lion before.
→ = A fox who had never seen a lion before, met him (a lion)

8) She keeps her ornaments in a safe. This is a safe place.
→ = She keeps her ornaments in a safe which is a safe place.

9) A cottager and his wife had a hen. The hen laid an egg every day. The egg was golden.
→ = A cottager and his wife had a hen which laid a golden egg every day.

10) The theft was committed last night. The man has been caught.
→ = The theft was committed last night by the man who has been caught.

11) The time was six o' clock. The accident happened then.
→ = The time was six o' clock when the accident happened.

12) He has many plans for earning money quickly. All of them have failed.
→ = He has many plans all of them which have failed for earning money quickly.

(3) Joining by turning one simple sentence into Adverbial Clause: In the following examples the Sub-ordinate Clause is made an Adverbial Clause:

13) I waited for my friend. I waited till his arrival.
→ = I waited for my friend until he came.

14) He fled somewhere. His pursuers could not follow him.
→ = He fled where his pursuers couldn't follow him.

15) Let men sow anything. They will reap its fruit.
→ = As men sow, as they reap.

16) He was not there. I spoke to his brother for that reason.
→ = As he was not there, I spoke to his brother.

17) We eat. We wish to live.
→ = We eat so that we may live.

18) Don't eat too much. You will be ill.
→ = If you eat too much you will be ill.

56. Exercise-3: **Combine each set of Simple Sentence into one Complex sentence:**

1) I wrote the letter. It contained the truth. He praised me for it.
2) Honesty is the best policy. Have you never heard it?
3) He came to see me. He wanted to tell something. His father was dead. He had been ill for a long time.
4) He took the medicine. He then felt better. It cured his headache.
5) He gave an order. He is obeyed. They fear to offend him.
6) Your conduct is very peculiar. I am unable to understand it.
7) He is sure to receive his pay. It is due to him. Why then does he worry?
8) His servants disliked him. They flattered him. He was very harsh to them.
9) The speed of the boat was remarkable. It was going against the current. it was going against the wind. These facts should be kept in mind.
10) The man talks most. The man does least. This very often happens.

Match your answers (of exercise-3)

1) I wrote the letter. It contained the truth. He praised me for it.
   - He praised me for the letter I wrote *which* contained the truth.
2) Honesty is the best policy. Have you never heard it?
   - Have you never heard *that* honesty is the best policy?
3) He came to see me. He wanted to tell something. His father was dead. He had been ill for a long time.
   - He *who* came to see me, wanted to tell something *that* his father *who* had been ill for a long time, was dead.
4) He took the medicine. He then felt better. It cured his headache.
   - *After* he took the medicine, he felt better *which* cured his headache.
5) He gave an order. He is obeyed. They fear to offend him.
   - *As* they fear to offend him, his order is always obeyed.
6) Your conduct is very peculiar. I am unable to understand it.
   - I am unable to understand your conduct *which* is very peculiar.
7) He is sure to receive his pay. It is due to him. Why then does he worry?
   - Why does he worry to receive his pay *which* is sure and due to him?
8) His servants disliked him. They flattered him. He was very harsh to them.
   - *As* he was very harsh to his servants, they disliked him and they flattered.

9) The speed of the boat was remarkable. It was going against the current. It was going against the wind. These facts should be kept in mind.
   - *Though* the boat was going against the current and wind, the speed of the boat was remarkable to keep in mind.

10) The man talks most. The man does least. This very often happens.
   - The man *who* talks most does least, happens very often.

6. Split-up of a Sentence

57. The term '**Split-up**' *is just the opposite of* '**Synthesis**' or joining of sentences. In split-up, we do split, i.e., separate or break up a sentence to make as far possible independent sentences (**not like:** what actually 'Analysis' does). In split-up, we try to give independent form to some essential or important parts of a sentence (i.e., **clauses, phrases, participle, adjective or adverb**, sometimes also the **infinitive, phrase in apposition, & Nominative Absolute, etc.**) are turned to be smaller independent simple sentences.

There are **three main ways to split up** a long sentence into various small simple sentences:

A. First, break up the sentence into Clauses as per Principal & Co-ordinate (in case of Compound Sentence);

or

B. Break up the sentence into Clauses as per Principal & Sub-ordinate (if the sentence is a Complex one). Try each of them to give independent sentence forms, removing the linkers, & borrowing some required words, like finite verbs (giving non-finite verbs the finite verb forms), &

C. Find out, if any, (in case of Simple Sentence or Single Clause)
   1) Participle or Adjective,
   2) Infinitive,
   3) Preposition with a Noun or Gerund,
   4) Noun or Phrase-in-Apposition,
   5) Nominative Absolute, or

6) Adverb or Adverbial Phrase— try to use them in different independent simple sentences in the following ways:

58. **For an example, study the following:**

(1) Everybody ***knows*** that the boy who ***came*** to me for help ***is*** a liar and a cheat.

In the above sentence, there are three finite verbs expressed—**knows, came** & **is**. They easily can be used in independent sentences. The underlined words are the linkers which are to remove (or not to use) in the new sentences.

If you notice carefully, you will find two adjectives— '***liar***' & '***cheat'***, connected by 'and'. We may also try to use two Adjectives in two different sentences; as,

→ A boy came to me for help.
→ He is a liar.
→ He is a cheat.
→ Everybody knows this.

Remember: Arrange the sequence of incidents properly & don't lose the sense of the whole.

Study more examples:

(2) Napoleon, the greatest of French soldiers; Wellington, the greatest of English Generals; and Nelson, the greatest of English Admirals, all heroes of their respective countries, were contemporaries.

After split up, the independent short simple sentences are-

→ Napoleon was the greatest of French soldiers.
→ Wellington was the greatest of English Generals.
→ Nelson was the greatest of English Admirals.
→ They were all heroes of their respective countries.
→ They were contemporaries.

In the above long sentence, we had four Phrases in Appositions (underlined), with one finite verb. The long sentence itself is a Simple sentence, is split up into five short simple sentences.

(3) Bassanio ***told*** Antonio that he ***wished*** to repair his fortune by marrying a lady whom he dearly ***loved*** and whose father, who has lately ***dead***, had ***left*** her sole heiress to a large estate.

After split up, the independent short simple sentences are-

→ Bassanio wished to repair his fortune by marrying a lady.
→ He loved her dearly.
→ Her father was lately dead.
→ He had left his heiress to a large estate.
→ Bassanio said all this to Antonio.

In the above long sentence, there are five clauses in total with five finite verbs, in bold. They are used in five independent sentences after the split up. The long sentence was a Complex one.

To be Noted: So, for split up, we have to hunt for **finite verbs** cum **clauses** as well as look for Participles or Adjectives, Adverb or Adverbial Phrase, Noun or Phrase in Apposition, Infinitive, use of Gerund, Nominative Absolute, etc. to form independent Sentences; as read more examples.

(4) Everybody admires the man who passed all the University examinations as a private student while working as a humble railway points man at a lonely station.

After split up:

1) Everybody admires the man.
2) He passed all the University examinations.
3) This he did as a private student.
4) He was working as a humble railway points man all this time.
5) His posting was at a lonely station.

In the above long sentence, the underlined are the adverbials- adv of manner, time & place. The three adverbials are used as three different sentences, (iii), (iv), & (v), while sentence (i) comes from principal clause and (ii) from the sub-ordinate clause.

(5) When Newton was fourteen years old, his mother's second husband being now dead, she wished her son to leave school and assist her in managing the farm **at Woolsthrope**.

After split up:

1) The second husband of Newton's mother was now dead.

2) Newton was fourteen years' old at that time.
3) She wished her son to leave the school.
4) She had a farm at Woolsthrope.
5) She wished him to help her in managing it.

In the above long sentence, the underlined is the use of **Absolute Phrase**, and the words **in bold is an example of adverbials, denoting place**. Both they have turned into sentences, (i) & (iv); while others have come from three clauses—Sub-ordinate, Principal & one Co-ordinate.

(6) I seem to myself like a child, playing on the sea-shore, and picking up here and there a curious shell or a pretty pebble, while the boundless ocean of Truth lies undiscovered before me.

After split up:

- The ocean of Truth lies before me.
- It is boundless.
- It lies undiscovered.
- Then, I seem to myself like a child.
- The child plays on the sea-shore.
- He picks up a curious shell from here and there.
- He picks up a pretty pebble.
-

Or, in this way:

- A child often plays on the sea-shore.
- He picks up here and there a curious shell.
- Or he picks up a pretty pebble.
- I seem to myself like such a child.
- The ocean of Truth lies before me.
- It is boundless.
- It lies undiscovered.

However, *1st series is better.* The above long sentence is a Complex Sentence with one Principal & One Sub-ordinate clause only. But in the sentence, there are **participle phrases which are used as phrase in apposition**—*'playing on the sea-shore'*, *'picking up here & there'*, two adjectives or participle words—*boundless & undiscovered*, two objects—*'a curious shell'* & *'a pretty pebble'*, and one adverbial *'before me'*. All they are used in separate sentences.

Split up through Analysis

- We said, '**split-up**' is the opposite term of '**Synthesis**', but not of '**Analysis**'. We can 'split-up' a sentence well, if we have first-hand knowledge of analysis. Let's see. Read the following sentences.

1. The other day my younger brother saw two men fighting each other.
2. The Judge, accepting the verdict of the jury, found the prisoner tremendously guilty.
3. On hearing of my misfortune, all my friends ran to my help.
4. An intelligent boy, the son of a very poor man, badly needs your help to be able to continue his studies.

In the Analysis, they are like:

Adjunct to Subject	Subject Proper	Finite Verb	Object with Adjectives	Partici ple/ Compl ement	Adverbial expansion
my younger	brother	saw	two men	fighting with each other	The other day
1) The 2) accepting the verdict of the jury	Judge	found	the prisoner	guilty	tremendous ly
1) all my 2) On hearing my misfortun e	friends	ran	----	----	to my help
1) An 2) intelligent 3) the son of a very poor man	boy	needs	your help	----	badly, to be able to continue his studies

Note

If you carefully study, you will find your necessary elements for split-up the sentences, mainly input (are) in the columns of Adjuncts to Subjects, attributes to object, complement/participle, & Adverbials.

You will find there— **Participle or Adjectives**, **Phrase-in-Apposition**, **Absolute Phrase**, **Complement** & **Adverbials** which are necessary for split-up or break up a sentence to make many independent short simple sentences.

Infinitive & **Gerund** are also important guides for split-up a sentence that we generally find in the columns of **Subjects, Objects**, or in the **adverbial expansion**.

For example, in sentence 1, *the **complement** & **adverbials***— both can be converted into independent simple sentences, *along with separate one for the main verb*.

In sentence 2, the ***phrase in apposition*** is in the Adjuncts to the Subject; that can be turned into independent simple sentence along with the *complement*, *adverbials*, & *main verb*.

In sentence 3, *the **preposition with gerund,*** *'On hearing'*, noted in the adjuncts to the subject, & *the object of the gerund 'my misfortune'* as well as others, like adjectives, adverbials—can separately be given simple sentence forms.

In sentence 4, the adjective, possessive, adverbials—can be broken down to form separate sentences borrowing suitable verbs and introductory subjects, **there, it** etc.

Thus, after split-up into Small Sentences:

1.
- It was another day.
- My younger brother saw two men.
- They were fighting with each other.

2.
- The jury passed a verdict. (The jury decided something on it.)
- The Judge accepted the verdict of the jury.
- He found the prisoner guilty.
- His guilt was tremendous.

3.
- I was in misfortune.
- My friends heard this.
- They all ran to me.
- They all wanted to help me.

4.
- There is a boy.

- He is intelligent. (The boy is intelligent.)
- But his father is very poor.
- The boy wants to continue his studies.
- He badly needs your help.

59. Split up of Complex Sentences: More examples:

1) When I was a student, I was one day taken to task by the Principal of my college for having played on behalf of an outside club, though he had ordered us not to do so.

2) Having been informed that my brother who had gone to Delhi to attend the Legislative Assembly was lying seriously ill of fever there, I applied for one week's leave of absence in order that I might go to him to arrange for proper treatment.

After Analysis into Clauses:

Clauses	Kind of Clause	Connectives
1/(a) I was one day...of an outside club (b) When I was a student (c) though he ...not to do so	Principal clause Sub. Adv. Clause, qualifying '**was taken** in (a)' Sub. Adv. Clause, qualifying '**having played** in (a)'	when though
2. (a) Having been **informed**, I **applied for** one week's leave of absence (b) That **my brother** was lying seriously ill of fever there (c) Who had gone to Delhi to attend the Legislative Assembly (d) In order that I might go to him to arrange for proper treatment.	Principal clause Sub- Noun Clause, object to verb '**informed**' in (a)' in participle form Sub. Adj. Clause, describing '**my brother**' in (b)' Sub. Adv. Clause, describing '**applied for**' in (a)'	that who In order that

We have now seven clauses in total after analyzing the above two complex sentences. What, if we now analyze further as Subject, predicate and to their adjuncts:

Adjunct to Subject	Subject Proper	Finite Verb	Object with Adj.	Complement	Adverbial Adjunct
	I	was taken	by the Principal of my college	to task	one day, for having playe on behalf of an outside club,
	I	was		a student	when
	He	had ordered	us		not to do so
having been informed	I	applied			for one week's leave of absence
my	Brother	was lying			seriously ill of fever there
	who	had gone			to Delhi to attend the L. Assembly
	I	might go			to him to arrange for proper treatment.

The Analysis is only to help you better understand about Split-up. Beyond that, it does not have connection with 'Split-up'. However, after split-up, the smaller simple sentences are, as the followings:

1. I was a student of a college.
2. The Principal had ordered us not to play for an outside club.
3. But I played on behalf of an outside club.
4. One day, the Principal sir took me before the task (commission).

1. My brother had gone to Delhi.
2. He went/was there to attend the Legislative Assembly.
3. He was lying ill of fever there.

4. It was serious.
5. I was informed of that.
6. I might go to him there.
7. I had to arrange for him proper treatment.
8. So, I applied for one week's leave of absence.

Split up of Complex Compound

60. **Split up of Complex Compound Sentences** (where at least two complex sentences (or two sub-ordinate clauses) are joined by a Co-ordinate Conjunction.)

1. Though I was ill I tried my best; **but** as ill luck would have it all my exertion ended in smoke.
2. Long ago, when I was yet a student I once went to Darjeeling, **where** (and there) I was charmed by the beautiful mountain scenery that greeted me on all sides.

If they are analyzed:

Clauses	Kind of Clause	Connectives
a) I tried my best	Principal clause	
b) Though I was ill	Sub. Adv. Clause, qualifying '**tried**' in '(a)'	Though
c) But all my exertion ended in smoke	Principal Clause, Co-ordinatc to '(a)'	but
d) As ill luck would have it	Sub. Adv. Clause, qualifying '**ended**' in '(c)'	as
a) Long ago, I once went to Darjeeling	Principal clause	
b) When I was yet a student	Sub- Adv. Clause, describing 'went' in (a)'	When
c) Where I was charmed by...scenery	Principal Clause, Co-ordinate to '(a)'	Where (**and there**)
	Sub. Adj. Clause, qualifying '**scenery**' in (c)'	that

d) That greeted
me on all sides

The New Simple Sentences will be like the followings:

1. I was ill.
2. Yet, I tried my best.
3. But it was my ill luck.
4. All my exertion ended in smoke.

1. It was long ago.
2. I was yet a student.
3. I went to Darjeeling.
4. The mountain was full of beautiful scenery.
5. It was on all sides.
6. I was charmed.

61. A Few Difficulties may arise in ***Analysis,*** but not in ***Split-up***. Study them attentively:

Split-up of 'Quoted Sentence', 'Parenthetic Phrase & Clause'

In case **"Quoted sentences": -**

He said, "I cannot come to you today. My brother is ill and I have to attend on him. You may, however, expect me tomorrow."

- **The quotation consists of three sentences**, which cannot be taken separately in their relation to the principal verb '**said**', but have to be treated as a single part of speech, **object** to the verb, **'said'**.
- The quotation has been taken in this case **as a long compound word**, a **noun equivalent**, object to the transitive verb 'said'; as, I said, "**I am ill**".
- I was surprised by his '**I don't care**' attitude (a **compound adjective** describing the noun, 'attitude').

In analysis, the above expressions, may arise difficulties. However, we can split -up them easily. Study the sentences, after split-up of the 'quotations':

a. **He said**, "I cannot come to you today. My brother is ill and I have to attend on him. You may, however, expect me tomorrow."

1) I cannot come to you today.

2) My brother is ill.
3) I have to attend on him.
4) You may, however, expect me tomorrow.
5) He said all these to me.

b. I said, "**I am ill**".
 1) I was ill.
 2) I said that to him.

c. I was surprised by his "**I don't care**' attitude".
 1) He had 'I don't care attitude'.
 2) I was surprised by that.

62. **Parenthetic Phrases:**
 a. He is, **to tell the truth**, not quite frank.
 b. I was, **to be frank**, much surprised.
 c. I am, **of me**, ok.

➤In all the above cases, the '**phrases within commas before & after**', are called '**Parenthetic Phrases**' and they can be analyzed separately and similarly can be taken out without injuring the sense. In the above sentences, they are used in Simple Sentences. Their split-ups are as the followings:
 a. He is, **to tell the truth**, not quite frank. = He is not quite frank. It is true.
 b. I was, **to be frank**, much surprised. = I was surprised. Frankly I like to say that.
 c. I am, **of me**, ok. = Are you asking about me? I am ok.

63. **More 'Parenthetic Expressions' for Split-up:**

 a. He is, **I am sure**, something like a poet.
 b. His conduct, **I believe**, is good.
 c. Why do you, my friend, **I don't know**, hate me?
 d. Why do you, **it is not clear**, not talk to me now-a-days?
 e. But you should, **I am likely agreed**, do so.
 f.

➤ All the above are simple sentences while the bold written words are **parenthetic expressions**, they are thrown into the main sentence, like a phrase in apposition or an Absolute Phrase. They can be analyzed separately. In the sentences they **are thrown in**

as independent elements; and they may be taken out without injuring the sense.

Study, how we can split up them:

a. He is, **I am sure**, something like a poet.
   - He is something like a poet. I am sure about that.

b. His conduct**, I believe**, is good.
   - His conduct is good. I believe so.

c. Why do you, my friend, **I don't know**, hate me?
   - I like address you as my friend. Why do you hate me? I don't know the reason.

d. Why do you, **it is not clear**, not talk to me now-a-days?
   - You are not talking with me now-a-days. What is the reason? /Why are you doing so? It is not clear to me.

e. But you should, **I am likely agreed**, do so.
   - But you should do. I am likely agreed to that.

f. I was surprised by his '**I don't care**' attitude.
   - He had 'I don't care' attitude. I was surprised by that.

When 'Parenthetic' expressions used in Compound

a. He is, **I am sure**, something of a poet & his poetry are too good to read by others.
b. His conduct,**I believe**, is good & too good to converse with.
c. Why do you, my friend, **I don't know**, give me light and snatch it away?
d. Why do you, it **is not clear**, begin to talk and stop forever?

- All the above are compound sentences with two principals while the bold written words are **parenthetic expressions**; they can be analyzed separately. In the sentences they **are thrown in as independent elements**; and they may be taken out without injuring the sense.

- Study their Split-up

a. He is, **I am sure**, something of a poet & his poetry are too good to read by others.
    - He is something of a poet. His poetry are too good to read by others. I am sure about that.
b. His conduct, **I believe**, is good & too good to converse with.
    - His conduct is good. But it is too good to converse with. I believe so.
c. Why do you, my friend, **I don't know**, give me light and snatch it away?
    - You give me light. And you snatch it away too. Why do you do all these with me? I don't know the reason of it.
d. Why do you, it **is not clear**, begin to talk and stop forever?
    - You begin to talk. And you stop it forever. Why do you do this? It is not clear.

When 'Parenthetic' expressions used in Complex

a. He is, **I am sure**, something of a poet who reads alone his poetry.
b. His conduct, **I believe**, is what is not suitable for his own age.
c. He is the man who, **I believe**, did it.
d. This is the boy who, **I think**, came the other day.

All the above are complex sentences with only one principal & one sub-ordinate clauses while the **bold written words are parenthetic expressions**; they can be analyzed separately.

❑ Split-up of Parenthetic expressions in Complex

a. He is, **I am sure**, something of a poet who reads alone his poetry.
    - He is something of a poet. He reads his poetry alone. I am sure about that.

b. His conduct, **I believe**, is what is not suitable for his own age.
    - He is of old age (i.e., old enough by age). His conduct does not suit to his age. I believe that.

c. He is the man who, **I believe**, did it.
    - Someone has done it. He is the man. I believe this.

d. This is the boy who, **I think**, came the other day.
    - A boy came the other day. This is the boy. I think that.

Use of 'It' & 'There' in Split-up

64. In split-up, **'there'**, **'it'** as introductory subjects are often required to introduce separate & simple sentences (besides other words & suitable finite verbs as necessary); as,

a. They went out in the raining. = **It** was raining. They went out **then** (during that time).

b. A man in the school was collapsed in heart attack. = **There** was a man in the school. He collapsed **there** in heart attack.

c. A king, named Ashoka ruled over Magadh in India. = **There** was a king. His name was Ashoka. **Once** he ruled over Magadha.

- As custom '**There**' is to fall in the group of an '**Adv. Adjunct';** but when they are used as **introductory subjects**, they lose the force to call anymore as Adverbial adjuncts.

- **'It'**, *as impersonal pronoun* **refers to any animal, child,** it also, often, mean any preceding or succeeding statement, a phrase, a clause, and even a sentence. (Study in details in the chapter of Pronouns).

d. **It** is easy ***to say so.***

→ You may say anything. It is easy.

e. **It** is hard ***to believe him.***

→ I can't believe him. It is very hard.

f. **It** is time ***to go now.***

→ The time has arrived. We should go now.

g. Two people were fighting in the field.

→ **There** were two peoples in the field. They were fighting.

h. Ashoka ruled India.

→ **There** was a king. His name was Ashoka. He ruled India.

65. If we have got mastery over analysis of sentences, and know its parts well, to identify and understand, **we are always free to do Split-up of Sentences directly (**without any analysis, as shown in the above through few pages.)

So, we can jump or return to the split-up in the direct mode or manner, as did earlier. Practice with some more examples:

1) When Newton was fifty years old and had been hard at work more than twenty years studying the theory of light, he one day went out of his chamber leaving his little dog asleep before the fire.
   a. Newton was now fifty years old.
   b. He had been hard at work more than twenty years.
   c. He had been studying the theory of light.
   d. One day he went out of his chamber.
   e. He left his little dog before the fire.
   f. It was asleep.

2) A right-minded man will have the courage to live honestly within his means; for he who incurs debts is in spirit a dishonest as the man who openly picks your pocket.
   a. A man may incur debts.
   b. Another man may openly pick your pocket.
   c. The former is dishonest in spirit like the latter.
   d. So, a right-minded man will live within his means.
   e. He has the courage to do so.

3) Everybody should learn how to swim because swimming is a fine exercise and is often the means of saving one's own life.
   a. Swimming is a fine exercise.
   b. It is often the means of saving one's own life.
   c. So, everybody should learn how to swim.

4) One morning when the giant was lying awake in bed, he heard some music, which sounded so sweet to his ears that he thought it to be the king's musicians passing by.
   a. One morning the giant was lying awake in bed.
   b. At that time, he heard some music.
   c. It sounded very sweet to his ear.
   d. He thought it to be the kings' musicians.
   e. They were supposed passing by.

66. **Exercise: Split up the followings into Simple sentences:**
   a. On a dark night Subhas Chandra Bose set out from home in disguise to escape into Germany where he wanted to organize a strong army to fight against the British.

b. As we reached the heritage building with the desire of visiting the interior, we found the building closed it being a scheduled weekly holiday and we felt much disheartened.
c. Hearing a girl crying for help, a youth plunged into the water and managed with great difficulty to bring her to shore.
d. Seeing that his end is near, Hamlet suddenly stabbed his uncle with the poisoned sword, and avenged at last the murder of his father.
e. A Metro Railway employee, Biswajit Biswas, pulled back a woman attempting to jump to her death at the Tallygunj station but fell off the edge of the platform himself and was killed.

You may check your answers of the above 'Exercise', here:

a. It was a dark night. Subhas Chandra Bose set out for home. He was in disguise. He was to escape into Germany. He wanted to organize a strong army there. The army was to fight against the British.
b. We reached the heritage building. We had a desire of visiting the interior. We found the building closed. It was a scheduled weekly holiday. We felt much disheartened.
c. A girl cried for help. A youth heard it. He plunged into the water. He managed to bring her to shore. He did it with great difficulty.
d. His end was near. Hamlet saw this. He stabbed his uncle suddenly with a sword. The sword was poisonous. He at last avenged the murder of his father.
e. It was at the Tallygunj station. A woman attempted to jump to her death. Biswajit Biswas was a Metro Railway employee. He pulled back the woman. He fell off the edge of the platform himself. He was killed.

7. Direct & Indirect Speech (Change of Narration)

67. **Narration:** The French derivative word, 'narration' means 'the act of recounting', which 'relates some action or occurrence' (i.e., 'to *tell somebody about something that you have experienced or already happened.*)

Speech: The English word, 'Speech', on the other hand, means 'a session of speaking'; 'a long oral message given publicly, usually by one person'. It also means for 'talk'.

So, let's see, both the terms mean for same thing, 'delivering an oral message' to a second or third person other than the speaker himself, while the speaker is in the first person. But who conveys the message or the message is speaking to, may be of any person.

Direct Speech & Indirect Speech

A speech can be delivered in two ways, **directly**, by quoting 'the exact words of the speaker' or **indirectly**, by 'delivering the message without using exact words of the speaker'.
Thus, we have –

i. **Direct Speech** (when we quote actual words of the speaker)
ii. **Indirect speech** (reporting or delivering the message without quoting exact words of the speaker.)

68. General Features of 'Direct Speech'

1. The Direct Speech is generally **put within inverted commas, single** or double ('...' /"...") and sometimes using colons (:).
2. The verb, generally placed before the quoted words is called the **reporting verb**. [However, the reporting verb can also be used after a quotation.]
3. We **use comma (,)** before the quoted speech.
4. The quoted speech **must begin with the capital** letter.
5. Sometimes, the subject & the reporting verb are placed after the quoted speech. In this case, verb comes first and then the subject.

Direct Speech looks like...

The student said, "I shall go to school."
Or
"I am very sorry to wake you up, sir," said the stranger.

Note the differences

- Rama said, 'I **am** very busy **now**.' (Direct speech)
- Rama said **that** he **was** very busy **then**. (Indirect speech)

❑What to be noted?

Let's Discuss...

- We use **inverted commas** in direct speech, of course to mark off the exact words of the speaker. In the indirect speech that is replaced with a linking word, **'that'**.
- The proper noun **'I'** is changed into **'he'**.
- The verb **'am'** in direct speech is changed to **'was'**.

- The adverb **'now'** is changed to **'then'.**

5 Major Rules of Narration Change

69. Study the **five major rules** of Narration Change that follows 'Narration Change of different kinds of sentences' along with some extra guidelines for each kind.

1) **Use of Linkers-** that, if/whether, wh- words or infinitive verb. See the chart:

	Linker or Conjunction	used, in case of the sentence is-
1	that	Assertive sentence
2	If/whether or wh- words	Interrogative
3	Infinitive/that	Imperative
4	That	Optative (Sentence of wish or prayer)
5	That	Exclamatory

Note: 'that' linker is often omitted in Spoken English; as,

He said to me, 'I don't believe you.'
He said he didn't believe me.

2) **Change of Tense** or **verb forms:** When reporting verb is in past tense, all present tenses of Direct Speech are generally changed into corresponding Past Tenses (with some exceptions); as see the table:

	Tense in D. Speech	Becomes/ change into	Tense in Ind. Speech
1.	Simple present	Change into	Simple past
2.	Present Continuous	,,	Past Continuous
3.	Present Perfect	,,	Past Perfect
4.	Present Perfect Continuous	,,	Past Perfect Continuous

5.	'Shall' of future	,,	Should
6.	'Will' of future	,,	Would or should
7.	Simple past	,,	Past perfect
8.	Past continuous	,,	Past perfect continuous

Exception (1): tenses may not be changed, if the statement is one universal truth or a habitual fact;

Or

If reporting verb is in present or future tense.

3) **Change in Person, Number, Case, Gender of Pronouns & Possessive Adjectives:** This change occurs in accordance to relation with the reporter and hearer. Carefully study the charts:

Note: '1st person in quoted speech changes to subject of reporting verb in the Indirect Speech;
2nd person changes to person spoken to;
&, there is no change in 3rd person.

Person in D.S.	Changes to	Person of Ind. Speech
1st person (I, we, me, us, my, our) of Direct Speech	Changes to	Person, Number, Gender, case of Subject of Reporting Verb

Prabir says to his uncle, '**I** am going to Kolkata tomorrow.'
> **Prabir** tells his uncle that **he (Prabir)** is going to Kolkata next day.

2nd person (You, your) of Direct Speech	Changes to	Person, Number, Gender, case of the person spoken to in the Direct Speech

Father said to **me**, '**You** should obey your teachers.'
> Father told **me** that **I** should obey our teachers.

There is no change in the third person.

You said, '**he** is a coward.' > You said that **he** was a coward. >You told him a coward.

4) Change in **Demonstrative Pronouns, & adverbs of time and place**: (Words expressing nearness in time, place or pronouns changes to words expressing distance.)

	Demonstrative Pronouns	Changes to	In Indirect Speech
1.	This	Change into	That
2.	these	,,	those
3.	That	Remain unchanged	That
4.	those	,,	those
5.	It (impersonal pronoun)	,,	it

Note-1: Study the below chart about **'the Adverbs of Time'**.

	Adverbs of Time in (Direct Speech)	Changes to	In Indirect Speech
1.	Now	Changes into	Then
2.	Today		That day
3.	Yesterday	,,	The day before/ the previous day
4.	Tomorrow	,,	The next day/ the following day
5.	Next day (week, month) etc.	,,	The following day (week, month, etc.)
6.	This day/night	,,	That day/night
7.	Last night	,,	The previous night/ the night before

8.	Ago	,,	before
9.	Hence (for this reason/from now)	,,	thence
10	Thence (for that reason/ from then/starting from that time)	Remained unchanged	thence
11.	thus	,,	In that way; /so
12.	The day before yesterday	,,	Two days before
13.	The day after tomorrow	,,	Two days after
14.	A year ago,	,,	A year before; the previous year

Note-2: Now, study the chart about **the Adverbs of Place**.

	Adverbs of Place in (Direct Speech)	Changes to	In Indirect Speech
1.	Here	Change into	There
2.	Hither (to this place)	,,	Thither (to/towards that place)
3.	There	Remain unchanged	there
4.	Thither	,,	thither
5.	Thence (from that place)	,,	thence

Note-3: 'Come' & 'go' may be interchanged with the narration change.
Note-4: These changes rely upon situation, time & place when or where the speaker speaks this, and thus they also may not change.

5) **Other Important Changes in Indirect Speech from Direct:**

Note: Vocatives are popular in imperative sentence.

	Other Changes from Direct Speech	Changes to	In Indirect Speech
1.	Says to/said to	Changes to	tells/told

The old man said to his son, “My son, you must not spoil your time.”
>The old man **<u>told his son affectionately</u>** that he must not spoil his time.

2.	In interrogative, linker	If/whether	is used.

He said, ‘Will you listen to such a man?’
> He **asked** them **whether** they would listen to such a man.

3.	In interrogative, linker	‘wh’ word	is used.

He said to me, ‘What are you doing?’
> He **asked** me **what** I was doing.

4.	In Imperative, urged,	request, advice, order	etc. is used.

He said, “Be quiet and listen to my words.”
> He **urged** them to be quiet and listen to his words.

5.	Exclaim in joy/sorrow	is used in	exclamatory

Alice said, “How clever I am!”
> Alice **exclaimed** that he is very clever.

Narration Change: Assertive Sentence

1) She says to me, “You told me, so I have done the work for you.”
→ She tells me that as I told her, so she has done the work for me.
2) Mrs. Bose said, “I take coffee daily in the afternoon.”
→ Mrs. Bose said that she takes coffee daily in the afternoon.
3) Rama said to me, “I drive very fast.”
→ Rama told me that he drives very fast.
4) “The weather is fine today,” the reporter said.

→ The reporter said that weather was fine that day.

5) "My mother cooks best," Ratna said to her friend.

→ Ratna told her friend that her mother cooks best.

6) He said, "My master is writing letters."

→ He said that his master was writing letters.

7) Sophia said, "I have passed the examinations."

→ Sophia said that she had passed the examinations.

8) "I know her address", said Gopi.

→ Gopi said he knows her address.

9) Father said, "Moon revolves round the earth."

→ Father said Moon revolves round the earth.

10) "English is easy to learn", said our teacher one day in the classroom.

→ One day in the classroom our teacher said that English is easy to learn.

11) He said, "I may go there."

→ He said that he might go there.

12) "My son leaves for Delhi tomorrow", father said.

→ Father said that his son would leave for Delhi the next day.

13) "You are very wicked; so, I shall not play with you", my friend said.

→ My friend told me that I am very wicked; so, she would not play with me.

14) I said to him, "The sky is blue."

→ I told him that the sky is blue.

15) "Father, if you put me into a good school, I shall be very glad.", said the little girl.

→ The little girl told her father that she would be glad if he would put her into a good school.

Narration Change: Interrogative

1) "Are you ill?" my father said to me.

→ My father asked If I was ill.

2) Shilpa said to her friend, "What are you doing?"

→ Shilpa wanted to know from her friend **what** she was doing.

3) My friend said to me, "When will you go home?"

→ My friend enquired of me when I should go home.

a. We replace reporting verbs of direct Speech with **'enquire'**, **'ask'**, **'want to'**, etc.

b. Linker—**if/whether** or **'Wh'** word 'is used.

c. In case of Yes/No type question, linker- **'if/whether'**, is used.
d. When a choice has to made or there is an alternate possibility, **'whether'** is preferred to use as linker.
e. **'Wh-'** word is used as linker when the reported speech is a 'Wh'- question.
f. **Question of direct speech changes to statement** or assertive sentence, and **we use full stop (.)** in place of question mark (?).
g. Other Rules are same as of Assertive Sentences.

4) She said to me, "Will you take tea or coffee?"
→ She asked me **whether** I would take tea or coffee.
5) "Are you coming with us?" my friend said to me.
→ My friend enquired of me **whether** I was going with them.
6) Robert said, "John is a good boy, is not he?"
→ Robert said that he assumed/thought John was a good boy.
→ Robert assumed John to be a good boy.
7) I said to Indira, "You can speak Hindi, can't you?"
→ I said to Indira that I thought she could speak Hindi.
→ I hoped Indira could speak Hindi.

h. In **case Narration Change of question tags**, the words— **assume**, **think**, **doubt**, **hope** or **believe**—may be used following an **infinitive** or as a separate verb after linker **'that'**.
i. **In such cases, if/whether are not used.**
j. *Such question tags are often said to be tentative statements, for speaker is not sure about the result or answer.* The speaker asks these questions for some assurance.

Narration changes of Question Tags:

8) The father said to his child, "You will do the task, won't you?"
→ The father told his child that he hoped he would do the task.
→ The father hoped his child to do the work.
9) "The officer did not agree to do that, did he?"
→ He said that he didn't believe that the officer had agreed to do that.
10) Ramesh said, "They will never return, will they?"
→ Ramesh said that he believed that they would not return.

Narration Change: Imperative

1. He said to me, "Please help me with a grammar book."
2. The father said to his son, "My boy, be brave and active."
3. "Samar, come in due time in the meeting," my boss said to me.
4. "Let's walk fast," said my friend.

➢**What did you notice in the sentences?**

They expressing...

1. He said to me, "Please help me with a grammar book." (...request)
2. The father said to his son, "My boy, be brave and active." (...advice)
3. "Samar, come in due time in the meeting at White Home," my boss said to me. (...order)
4. "Let's walk fast," said my friend. (...suggestion)

Notes

✓ The direct speeches expressing either ***order***, or ***request***, or ***advice***, or a ***suggestion***. They are called *imperative sentences.*

✓ The change of Imperative sentences from direct to indirect speech are almost same as we did in assertive sentences, except the followings:

We may use different reporting verbs to express the imperative mood:

Rules of Narration Change: Imperative Sentences

Rule No-1:

The reporting verbs are changed into—**order, request, advice**, or **suggest/propose** & others.

To express request, order or advice, '**tell**' or '**ask**'—may also be used sometimes when imperative mood is uncertain or rise any doubt in you about which word should to be used.

Note: See the matrix of words, expressing Imperative Mood:

imperative mood expressing words/verbs	Meanings
Order	Tell somebody to do something
Request	Ask for something politely
Advise	To tell somebody what you think they should do

Command	Give instruction to do something, generally in force or military
Beg/implore	Ask for something anxiously, for you need it very much
Entreat	Asking for something to do or to have in a serious & often in emotional way/ earnestly request someone
Urge/encourage	Advise or to try hard to persuade somebody to do something
Bid	To offer to do work/ provide a service/offer to pay, /attempt
Forbid	Order somebody not to do something
Warn	Strongly advise somebody to do or not to do something
Remind	Help somebody to remember something

Rule No-2:
To express the imperative mood, i.e., verbs of reported speech often changed into **infinitive.**

1) My friend said to me, "Go home at once."
→ My friend **advised** me to go home at once.
2) Tina said to me, "Please help me with a grammar book."
→ Tina **requested** me to help her with a grammar book.
3) The teacher said, "Silence."
→ The teacher **ordered** us to be silent.
4) I said to him, "Excuse me sir."
→ I **begged** him to excuse me.
5) "March on," said the general.
→ The General **commanded** his soldiers to march on.
6) "Don't forget to bring the medicine," he said to me.
→ He **reminded** me to bring the medicine.
7) "Please, please don't go on election duty," said my wife.
→ My wife **begged/implored** me not to go on election duty.
8) "Don't go near the fire, boys," said the officer.
→ The officer warned the boys not to go near the fire.
9) "Come in," she said to me.
→ She invited me to go in.
10) "Go on, try once again," said Parimal.

→ Parimal urged/encouraged me to try once again.

11) The old man said to the officer, “Please sir, pass my file.”

→ The old man entreated the officer to pass his file.

Some Questions or Exclamation in form, express also Imperative mood, like **command** or **request**, and they follow imperative structure to change the narration.

12) “Will you keep quiet!” the teacher said to the students.

→ The teacher bade/told/ordered the students to keep quiet.

13) “Would you lend me your book, please?”

→ He requested me to lend him my book.

14) “Would you show me you ticket please?”

→ The ticket checker asked the passenger to show his ticket.

Important Notes:

✓ Sometimes, the **subject** & the **reporting verb** are placed after the quoted speech. In this case, generally the verb comes first and then the noun subject. But if it is pronoun subject or the reporting verb has an object and others, it follows normal syntax. (subject +verb +object +others)

✓ Question (?), exclamation (!), or Comma (,) are used as necessary before end of quotation and & use Full stop (.) at the end of the statement.

✓ **First letter of the quotation or first letter of the sentence must be in capital but first letter after quotation is not bound to be capital.**

Imperative mood may also exit in the form of Question tags, like Question and exclamation:

15) “Close the door, won’t you?” he said to me.

→ He asked/requested me to close the door. (The question tag— ‘won’t you’—has been left out.)

16) “You should go home, don’t you?”

→ He advised me to go home.

Question Tags in Direct Speech of imperative sentence, where unnecessary to change, are generally left out in the Indirect Speech.

Read also the following:

Note: In interrogative sentences, in case of question tags, we have used the verbs—'doubt', think, hope, assume, believe, etc. The verbs are not necessary in the imperative mood in question tags. Normal imperative verbs should be used; **a request, order, advice**, etc.

Use of Vocatives in Imperative:

For Changing Direct Speech into Indirect:

a) **Read the table:**

	Other Changes from Direct Speech	Changes to	In Indirect Speech
1.	My boy/ My son/My dear	Changes into	Affectionately/ with affection

The old man said to his son, "My son, you must not spoil your time."
>The old man **told his son affectionately** that he must not spoil his time.
>The old man **affectionately advised** his son **not to spoil** his time.
The Old man **forbade his son with affection to waste** his time.

2.	Sir, please	Are replaced with	Kindly, Politely/Respectfully/ with respect

The clerk said to his boss, "Please excuse my fault, sir, for this time."
>The clerk **respectfully requested** his boss to excuse his fault for that time.

3.	**If 'Proper nouns' are used in address, in the Direct speech**	They become	**Objects of the verbs in Indirect Speech**

He said, "Samir, do the work for me please."
>He requested **Samir** to do the work for **him**.

4.	Some words like **'friends, 'gentlemen', 'countrymen'**	Changes to	**Addressing them as...**

The leader said, "**My brothers and sisters**, give me your votes."
>**Addressing them as** brothers and sisters, the leader appealed to people for their votes.
>The leader, **addressing people as his brothers and sisters,** appealed for vote.

> **Addressing them as his brothers and sisters**, the leader requested to people to give their votes.

b) In Some cases, **Vocatives should be avoided,** where it is not necessary:

c) Use of Not: In the Indirect Speech of the negative imperative sentence, **'not' is placed just before the infinitive verb, or use 'forbid'**

When '**forbid'** is used, **'not'** is not used.

5. If 'vocatives' are casual in use, avoid them in Indirect speech.

- I said to him, "Excuse me sir."
- ✓ I begged him to excuse me.
- The father said to his boy, "Do not run in the sun."
- ✓ The father advised his boy not to run in the sun.
- ✓ The father forbade his boy to run in the sun.

Use of 'Let' in the Narration Change

1) He said to me, "Let us go home."

→ He **suggested** to me that we **should** go home.

2) I said to my friend, "Let us have some music."

→ I **proposed** to my friend that we **should** have some music.

Note-1:

a. In the Direct Speech, when '**Let**' expresses a proposal or suggestion, use '**propose**', or '**suggest**' as the reporting verb.

b. Use '**should**' for 'Let' after subject of reported speech.

c. Use linker, '**that'**

3) "Let her do whatever she likes," her father said.

→ Her father ***said*** that she ***might do*** whatever she liked.

4) He said, "Let me come in."

→ He ***requested*** that he ***might be allowed*** to come in.

5) He said, "Let me have some milk."
→ He **wished** that she ***might have*** some milk.

Note-2:

a. But when 'Let' in the Direct Speech does not express a proposal it should be changed into '**might**' or '**might be allowed**' or into some other form according to the sense.
b. 'Might be allowed' is followed by an '**infinitive verb** in the indirect speech.
c. However, 'might' follow only simple tense of the verb in the indirect speech.
d. Use linker, '**that**'

Narration Change: Optative

Rule No-1: As an Optative Sentence express **wish** or **prayer,** the reporting verbs will be changed into
(***Wish, Pray, desire, Hope, bless***, or ***yearn***)

Know their meanings:

The verbs to be used in Indirect speech	Their meanings
Wish	Want something to happen; Want something to be true, even though it is unlikely or impossible.
Pray	Ask for help; Hope very much that something will happen.
Desire	Wish for something; Want something
Hope	Want something to happen & think it is possible.
Bless	Ask God to protect somebody;
Yearn	Long; want something very much, especially when it is very difficult to get.

Rule No-2: The conjunction **'that'** is used.

Rule-3: The optative sentence changed into assertive in the Indirect Speech.

Note: The person spoken to in the Direct Speech is omitted in the Indirect Speech.

Examples

1) The old man said to me, "May God bless you."
→ The old man prayed that God might bless me.
2) The old woman said to me, "May you live long."
→ The old woman wished that I might live long.
3) The holy man said, "May holy spirit rest upon you."
→ The holy man wished (or prayed) that holy spirit might rest upon me.
4) The old priest said to me, "May you succeed."
→ The old priest wished that I might succeed.

Narration Change: Exclamatory

Rule No-1: As the Direct Speech expresses an outburst of **'grief'**, **'joy'**, **'shame'**, etc. the reporting verbs must be changed into...

See the matrix with their meanings:

The verbs to be used in Indirect speech	Their meanings
Exclaim/ cry out	**Say something suddenly and loudly**, especially because of strong emotion or pain.
Applaud	**To show your approval of somebody or** something by clapping hands or making any sound.
Swear	**Make a serious promise** to do something; Use rude or offensive language, when you are angry of something.
Welcome/Bid	**Wish someone tenderly** by wishing good morning, good afternoon, /Good bye, etc.
Bless	Ask God to protect somebody;
Congratulate	Tell somebody that you are pleased about her success and achievement.

Confess /repent	Admits own faults

Rule No-2: The interjections or exclamations will be changed into words as shown in the matrix and they are used with the preceding reporting verbs:

See the matrix with their meanings:

The Interjections, used in the D.S.	**As they will be changed into:**
Alas!	Expressing sorrow or grief **(Exclaim with grief / sorrow; exclaim sadly)**
Hurrah!	Expressing delight or joy **(Cry out/exclaim in joy/ with delight)**
Bravo!	Applauding or praising somebody **(applaud +object +saying that +...)**
By Jove	Swearing...due to any cause **(Swear by Jove)**
What a / How...	Used in sorrow, grief, or in praise of something. (What or how will change to **'great' or 'very'**) & reporting verb would be as: **(Exclaimed in wonder/ exclaimed in pain,** etc.)
Fie!	Expressing disgust ((Exclaim in disgust) (Expressed his disgust and said that.../ Exclaimed that it was shameful & said)
Poor fellow!	Feel pity for someone (Pitied the man and exclaimed that...)
So, help me Heaven!	Pray to God (Prayed to Heaven to help him and resolved not to /to do something)
Who knew...!	(He said that none knew...)

Good gracious! Good Heavens!	Expressing joy (Exclaim with wonder) (Exclaim with delight)
Good Morning /Good bye	Wishing someone tenderly (welcome / bid)

Note: Normally **'great'** is placed before a **noun**; and **'very'** is placed before an **adjective.**

1) He said, "What a fool I am!"
→ He **cried out with grief** that he was a great fool.
2) The Giant said, "How selfish I have been!"
→ The Giant **confessed with regret** that he had been very selfish.
→ The Giant **repented** that he had been very selfish.
3) The children said to each other, "How happy we are here!"
→ The children **cried out with joy** saying to each other that they were very happy then.
4) The children said to each other, "How happy we were there!"
→ The children **felt sorrow** saying to each other that they had been very happy there.

Rule No-3: The conjunction **'that'** is used.

Rule-4: the exclamatory sentence changed into assertive in the Indirect Speech.

Note: The person spoken to in the Direct Speech may be used or omitted in the Indirect Speech, as it suits to.

The reporting verbs- **'welcome'**, **'wish'**, **'bid'** & **'congratulate'**— may also be used in the exclamatory sentence.

5) The host said to me, "Good Morning!"
→ The host **welcomed me wishing** good morning.
→ The host **wished** me good morning.
6) They said to the departing friends, "Good Bye, Our friends!"
→ They **bade** good bye to their friends.
7) They said to the invitees, "Welcome!"
→ They **bade** welcome to the invitees.
8) He said, "Congratulation, my friend!"
→ He congratulated his friend.

Note: The verb, **'Wish'** also comes with an optative sentence.

Reporting of 'One-word Replies' & 'Multiple Sentences'

One-word replies— **'yes'**, **'no'**, **'yesterday'**, **'tomorrow'**, **'today'**, **'surely'**, etc.—are found in dialogues or conversations.

1) She said to me, "Do you know the boy who recites so nicely?" I replied, "**No.**"
   → She asked me if I knew the boy who recited so nicely. I replied that ***I did not know him***. (Or ***I did not***.)

2) She asked me, "Will you take a cup of coffee?" I said, "**Yes.**"
   → She asked me whether I would take a cup of coffee. I replied that ***I would take***. (Or ***I would***.)

When one-word replies are converted into Indirect Speech, they **must be in complete sentences** (in terms of the preceding statements or questions) as shown in the examples:

More Examples

3) "When will you go to Burdwan?" I said to him. "**Tomorrow**", he replied.
   → I asked him when he would go to Burdwan. He replied that ***he would go (there) next day***.
4) "When did you come?" She asked me. "**Yesterday**", I said in reply.
   → She asked me when I had gone (there). I replied that ***I had gone yesterday.***
5) "Will you join us in the picnic?" They asked. (Question) "Surely", I said.
   → They asked me if I would join then in the picnic. I said that ***sure I would join them.*** (***Surely, I would***)
   → They invited me to join in the picnic. **I assured them of my joining.**

Reporting Multiple Type of Sentences in one frame:

6) I said to the boy, "Who are you? Whom do you want?"

→ I asked the boy who he was and whom he wanted.

7) Sanchita said to Kusum, "I don't feel well. I think you will not mind if I do not go to school today. Perhaps you will submit the project for me."

→ Sanchita **informed** Kusum that she *felt unwell (didn't feel well)*, and **hoped** that she would not mind if she *did not go to (remained absent from)* school that day. She **also said** that **perhaps** she (Kusum) would submit the project for her (Sanchita).

What to do:

Rule No-1: if the sentences are of same kind, one reporting verb can be used & other Reported Speeches may be added to each other by Conjunctions, like: **'and', 'or', 'but',** as the case may be:

8) Sergeant (to man): Stop! Didn't I tell you to stop? You can't go there.

Note: Look, the speech of the Sergeant is the combination of ***Exclamatory, Interrogative & Assertive sentences***. So, to turn this speech into Indirect, one Reporting verb is not sufficient, at least three reporting verbs are needed to convey three moods of the speaker.

→ The sergeant **ordered** the man to stop. He, then, **angrily asked** the man if he (the sergeant) had not told him (the man) to stop. The sergeant **also told** him that he (the man) could not go there.

What to do:

Rule No-2: if the sentences are of different kinds, separate reporting verbs are used in the Indirect Speech for them.

8. The Conversion or Transformation of Sentences

70. This Chapter includes the Conversion or Transformation of Sentences from **One** kind to **another** (what we have already learnt or discussed in the previous chapters) **& vice-versa**. So, in the

sense, it is just like compilation of that knowledge, and apply to for practice as through revision of the earlier ones. From practical sense, here is nothing new to discover.

A learner (when we are here, we might consider, he) **has already learnt –**

a. That a word can be used in different Parts of Speech, by derivative or without derivative;
b. That a phrase can be extended into a clause & a clause can be contracted into a phrase (simple to complex & compound, and vice-versa);
c. That a sentence can be written in different tenses;
d. That a sentence can be made with or without comparison;
e. That a sentence can be expressed in different voice (Active or Passive), moods or in manner of expression as well as in a different narration; (from Direct to Indirect & vice-versa) and thus, like many others.

Let's begin this 'chapter of conversion' with an adverb **'too'**, when 'too' can be expressed in other means or approach.

Conversion of Adverb 'too'

71. Conversion of Adverb '**too**'

Generally, we can replace the word **'too'**, with others like **'very'**, **'so'**, along with other changes in the sentence or inclusion of words, as shown below (Sl. No-1):

1) The news is **too** good. = The news is **very** good.
2) The news is **too** good to be true.
→ The news is **so** good *that it can't be* true.
3) These mangoes are **too** cheap to be good.
→ These mangoes are **so** cheap *that they can't be* good.
4) He drove **too** fast for the police to catch.
→ He drove **so** fast *that the police couldn't catch* him.
5) It is never **too** late to mend.
→ It is not **so** late *that it can't be* mended.
6) He is **too** ignorant for a postman.
→ He is **so** ignorant *that he is not suitable candidate* for a postman.
7) You are **too** late to hear the first speech.
→ You are **so** late *that you couldn't hear* the first speech.

8) My heart is **too** full for words.
→ My heart is **so** full *that I am eager to say* many words.
9) She was sobbing **too deeply** to make any answer.
→ She was sobbing **so much** *that she can't make* any answer.
10) She is **too** proud to beg pardon.
→ She is **so** proud *that she can't beg* pardon.
11) He is **far too** stupid for such a difficult post.
→ He is **so much** stupid *that he is not suitable* for such a difficult post.
12) He speaks **too fast** to be understood.
→ He speaks **so fast** *that he cannot be understood* by others.
13) This tree is **too high** to climb.
→ The tree is **so high** *that you can't* climb.
14) The bag was **too heavy** for me to carry.
→ The bag was **so heavy** *that I couldn't* carry.
15) The shirt is **too small** for him.
→ The shirt is **so small** *that he can't* wear.
16) The work is **too much** for any man to do single-handed.
→ The work is **so much** *that no a single man can do* it.
17) The fact is **too evident** to require any proof.
→ The fact is **so much evident** *that it doesn't need* or require any proof.

Conversion of Degrees (adj. & adv.)

72. 'Degrees' or 'Forms of Comparison occur to Adjective and Adverb, and one form of comparison can be change to other. Study the examples:
(From positive to comparative, superlative & vice versa. (Sl. No-2))

1) I am as strong as him.
- He is not stronger than me.
- None of us is the strongest. Who is the strongest here? (Answer will be 'None' = No one)

2) This razor is not as sharp as that one.
- That razor is sharper than this one. Or, 'This razor is less sharp than that one.'
- That razor is one of the sharpest.

3) Few historians write as interestingly as Joshi.
- Joshi writes more interestingly than most historians.
- Joshi is one of the few historians who write most interestingly.

4) No other metal is as useful as iron.
   - Iron is more useful than any other metal.
   - Iron is the most useful of all metals.

5) India is the largest democracy in the world.
   - No other democracy in the world is as large as India.
   - India is larger than any other democracy in the world.

6) Mumbai is one of the richest cities in India.
   - Mumbai is richer than most other cities in India.
   - Very few cities in India are as rich as Mumbai.

7) Burza Khalifa is not only the tallest building in the world. (superlative)
   - Burza Khalifa is one of the tallest buildings in the world. (superlative)
   - Burza Khalifa is not taller than few other buildings in the world. (comparative)
   - Few other buildings in the world may be taller than Burza Khalifa. (comparative)
   - Few other buildings in the world are at least as tall as Burza Khalifa. (positive)
   - Burza Khalifa is perhaps not as tall as few other buildings in the world. (positive)

8) Peter is not one of the cleverest boys in the class.
   - Some boys in the class are cleverer than Peter.
   - Peter is less clever than some other boys in the class.
   - Peter is not so clever as some other boys in the class.

9) No other grammar book is as popular as of Peter's 'Complete English Grammar'.
   - Peter's 'Complete English Grammar' is more popular than any other grammar book.
   - Peter's 'Complete English Grammar' is the most popular of all grammar books.

10) It is better to starve than beg.
   - Begging is not as good as Starvation.
   - Starvation may be the best of all things like begging. (Begging is one of the worst things.)

11) He loves all his sons equally well.
   - No son he loves better than all others.
   - There is no son he loves the best / most.

12) Some beans are at least as nutritious as meat.
   - Meat is not more nutritious than some beans.
   - Meat is not the most nutritious comparing to some beans.

13) The airplane flies faster than birds.
   - No bird can fly as fast as an airplane.
   - An airplane flies the fastest among all birds.

14) Helen of Troy was more beautiful than any other woman.

- No woman was as beautiful as Helen of Troy.
- Helen of Troy was the most beautiful woman.

15) This newspaper has a bigger circulation than any other morning paper.

- No any other morning paper has as circulation as this newspaper.
- This newspaper has the biggest circulation among all morning papers.

Conversion of Active & Passive

73. A sentence in the Active form can be changed into the Passive form, and vice-versa (Sl. No-3):

1) Brutus stabbed Caesar.
   - Caesar was stabbed by Brutus.
2) The people made Gopal their king.
   - Gopal was made king by the people.
3) Who taught you grammar?
   - By whom was you taught grammar?
4) The Principal gave him a reward.
   - He was rewarded by the Principal.
5) The Romans expected to conquer Carthage.
   - Carthage was expected to be conquered by the Romans. / It was expected Carthage would be won (conquered) by the Romans.
6) One should keep one's promise.
   - One's promise should be kept.
7) I know her. = *She is known to me.*
8) I know the girl, Rossie by her name.
   - The girl, Rossie by her name, is known to me.
9) The police were taking me to prison.
   - I was being taken to prison by the police.
10) Her behavior vexes me often.
    - I am often vexed by her behavior.
11) It is time to shut up the shop.
    - It is time for the shop to be shut up.
12) The mayor's speech was loudly cheered.
    - The audience loudly cheered the mayor's speech.
13) Someone has picked my pocket.

- My pocket has been picked.

14) Our army has been defeated.
- The enemy has defeated our army.

15) I shall be obliged to go. = Duty will oblige me to go.
16) People admire the brave and honest.
- The brave and honest are admired by people.

17) Who taught you such tricks all this?
- By whom were you taught such tricks that all?

18) Brutus accused Caesar of ambition.
- Caesar was accused of ambition by his friend Brutus.

19) One expects better behavior from a college student.
- It is expected better behavior from a college student.

20) They showed a video of 'Titanic'. = A video of Titanic was showed.
21) You must endure what you cannot cure.
- What cannot be cured must be endured.

22) He made me do the work. = I was forced to do the work.
23) Nature teaches beasts to know their friends.
- Beasts are taught to know their friends by nature.

24) We expect good news from her. (We are expecting...)
- Good news is being expected from her.

25) He showed me the greatest respect.
- I was showed the greatest respect (by him).

26) Alas! We shall hear his voice no more.
- Alas! His voice will not be heard any more.

27) Shall I ever forget those happy days?
- Should those happy days be forgotten ever?

28) Do you not understand my meaning?
- Isn't my meaning understood? /Is my meaning not understood?

29) We must listen to his word. = *His words must be listened to.*
30) He pretended to be a Baron. (He was pretending...)
- He had been pretending to be a Baron.

31) You never hear of a happy millionaire. = It is never be heard of a happy millionaire.
32) The public will learn with astonishment that war is imminent.
- It will be learnt with astonishment that war is imminent.

33) Did you never hear that name? = Was it not heard that name (by you)?
34) Without effort nothing can be gained. = If you don't effort, you will gain nothing.
35) He was a chosen leader. = We chose him our leader.
36) By whom was this jug broken? = Who broke this jug?
37) I was offered a chair. = He (/They) offered me a chair.
38) This question will be discussed at the meeting tomorrow.

- I will discuss this question at the meeting tomorrow.

39) He will be greatly surprised if he is chosen.

- If we choose him, it will surprise him greatly.

40) He was arrested on a charge of theft, but for lack of evidence he was released.

- Police arrested him on a charge of theft, but for lack of evidence they released him.

Conversion from Affirmative to Negative

74. Study the following examples for the conversion of Affirmative sentence to Negative, and vice-versa (Sl. No-4):

1) As soon as he came, he made objections.
→ No sooner had he come, he made objections.
2) These fishing nets are all the wealth I own.
→ I own wealth nothing except these fishing nets.
3) I always love my motherland as a child loves her mother.
→ I always love my motherland no less than as a child to her mother. / There is hardly any difference of my love to my motherland and a child's to her mother.
4) Brutus loved Caesar.
→ Brutus had nothing but love for Caesar.
5) I was doubtful whether it was you.
→ I was not sure that it was you.
6) Old fools surpass all other fools in folly.
→ There is no fool like an old fool.
7) He is greater than me.
→ I am not so great as him.
8) Alfred was the best king that ever reigned in England.
→ No other king as good as Alfred ever reigned in England.
9) Everest is the highest mountain in the world.
→ No any other mountain is as high as the Everest.
10) He is sometimes foolish. = *He is not always wise.*
11) He failed to notice me when he came in.
→ He didn't notice me when he came in.
12) He was more rapacious than a griffin.
→ A griffin was not more rapacious than him.
13) He was as rapacious as a griffin. = He was not less griffin than rapacious.
14) Ashoka was the greatest king of the Maurya.

→ No other king of the Maurya was as great as king Ashoka.

15) Ashoka was greater than Chandra Gupta Maurya.

→ Chandra Gupta Maurya was not greater than king Ashoka.

16) The rose by any other name would smell as sweet.

→ No any other name of rose would lessen its smell as sweet.

17) Everybody will admit that he did his best. = Nobody will deny that he did the best.

18) Only a millionaire can afford such extravagance. = None but a millionaire can afford such extravagance.

19) Every man makes mistake sometimes and that defines his life.

→ There is none who does not make mistake and that doesn't define his or her life.

20) I care little what he says about me. = I do not care much what he says about me.

21) As soon as he saw me, he came up and spoke to me.

→ No sooner had he seen me he came up and spoke to me.

22) He must have seen the Taj Mahal when he went to Agra.

→ It is hardly possible that he has not seen the Taj Mahal when he went to Agra.

23) Nobody was absent. = Everybody was present.

24) None lives immortal. = Everybody is mortal.

25) No one can deny that she is pretty.

→ Everybody admits that she is pretty.

26) God will not never forget the cry of humble.

→ God will always remember the cry of humble.

27) I am not a little tired. = *I am tired very much.*

28) There was no one present who did not cheer.

→ Everybody was present there cheered.

29) I never in my life laid a plan and failed to carry it out.

→ I always in my life laid a plan and succeeded to carry it out.

30) Not many men would be cruel and unjust to a cripple.

→ Few men would be cruel and unjust to a cripple.

31) No man could have done it better.

→ Hardly a man could have done it better.

32) The two brothers are not unlike each other.

→ The two brothers are like each other.

33) The two brothers are not like each other.

→ The two brothers are unlike each other.

34) He has promised never to touch wine again.

→ He has promised to keep off ever from wine.

35) We did not find the road very bad.

→ We found the road on average condition.

36) There is no smoke without fire.

→ There is hardly any smoke without fire.

37) It is not likely that he will ever see his home again.

→ It is unlikely that he will ever see his home again.

Conversion of Interrogative to Assertive

75. The following are about the conversion of sentences, Interrogative to Assertive and vice-versa (Sl. No-5):

1) What though we happen to be late?

✓ It does not matter much though we happen to be late.

2) Why waste time in reading trash?

✓ It is foolish to waste time in reading trash.

3) Were we sent into the world simply to make money?

✓ We were not sent into the world simply to make money.

4) How can man die better than facing fearful odds?

✓ Man cannot die better than facing fearful odds.

5) When can their glory fade?

✓ Their glory can never fade.

6) Was he not a villain to do such a deed?

✓ He was a villain to do such a deed.

7) No one can be expected to submit for ever to injustice.

✓ Who expects to submit for ever to injustice?

8) There is nothing better than a busy life.

✓ Is there anything better than a busy life?

9) Nowhere in the world will you find a fairer building than the Taj Mahal.

✓ Where will you find a fairer building than the Taj Mahal?

10) It is useless to offer bread to a man who is dying of thirst.

✓ Is not it useless to offer bread to a man who is dying of thirst?

11) We could have done nothing without your help.

✓ What could we have done without your help?

12) That was not an example to be followed.

✓ Was that an example to be followed?

13) What though the field be lost?

✓ Nothing would be even if the field be lost.

14) Is that the way a gentleman should behave?

✓ That is not the way a gentleman should behave.

15) Who does not know the owl?

✓ Everyone knows the owl.

16) Shall I ever forget those happy days?

✓ I shall not ever forget those happy days.

17) Who is so wicked as to amuse himself with the infirmities of extreme old age?

✓ There is no one so wicked to amuse himself with the infirmities of extreme old age.

18) Why waste time in this fruitless occupation?

✓ We should not waste time in this fruitless occupation.

19) Is this the kind of dress to wear in public?

✓ This is not the kind of dress to wear in public.

20) Can you gather grape from thorns or figs from thistles?

✓ You cannot gather grape from thorns or figs from thistles.

Conversion of Exclamatory to Assertive

76. The following are about the conversion of sentences, from Exclamatory to Assertive and think vice-versa (Sl. No-6):

1) How sweet the moonlight sleeps upon this bank!

✓ The moonlight very sweetly sleeps upon this bank.

2) If only I were young again!

✓ I wish I were young again.

3) Alas! That youth should pass away!

✓ It is sad to think that youth should pass away.

4) How beautiful is night!

✓ Night is very beautiful.

5) To think of our meeting here!

✓ It is strange that we should meet here.

6) O what a fall was there, in my nature and sense!

✓ There was a great fall in my nature and sense.

7) How cold you are!

✓ You are very cold.

Transform the followings into Exclamatory:

8) It is very horrible night.

✓ How horrible night is it!

9) It was extremely base of him to desert you in your time of need.

✓ What a base of him to desert you in your need of time!

10) It is hard to believe that he did such a deed.

✓ Unbelievable! he did such a thing!

11) I wish I had met you ten years ago.

✓ If I had met you ten years ago!

12) It is very stupid of me to forget your name.
✓ How stupid I am to forget your name!
13) He leads a most unhappy life.
✓ What an unhappy life he leads!
14) I wish I had come one hour ago.
✓ If only I had come one hour earlier!
15) Ah, what a sight was there! = *There was very beautiful sight.*
16) What a piece of work is man! = A man is a wonderful piece of work.
17) What a wonderful creature an elephant is!
✓ An elephant is a very wonderful creature.
18) How awkwardly he manages his sword!
✓ He manages his sword very awkwardly.
19) O that we two were infants playing!
✓ I wish we were two infants playing.
✓ I wish we were two infants again and play together.
20) If only I had the wings of a dove! = I wish I had the wings of a dove.
21) If only I knew more of this! = I wish I knew more of this.

Conversion of Parts of Speech

77. Study the following examples of conversion of parts of speech used in the sentences (Sl. No-7):

1) That kind of joke does not ***amuse*** me. (verb)
✓ That kind of joke does not give me any ***amusement.*** (noun)
2) It ***costs*** twelve rupees. (verb) = The ***cost*** is twelve rupees. (noun)
3) He has ***disgraced*** his family. (verb)
✓ He is a ***disgrace*** to his family. (noun)
4) He ***fought bravely***. (verb, adv)
✓ He put up a ***brave fight.*** (Adj, noun)
5) The treaty of Salbai should be ***remembered*** as one of the landmarks in the history of India. (verb)
✓ The treaty of Salbai is worthy of ***remembrance*** as one of the landmarks in the history of India. (noun)
6) I cannot ***consent*** to your going. (verb)
✓ I cannot give my ***consent*** to your going. (noun)
7) He gave a ***curt reply.*** (adj. noun) = He ***replied curtly***. (verb, adv)
8) He showed ***generosity*** even to his enemies. (noun)
✓ He was ***generous*** even to his enemies. (adjective)
9) There is ***slight difference*** between the two shades. (adj. & noun)

- ✓ The two shades are ***slightly different.*** (adv., adj.)

10) The act made them ***free***. (adjective)

- ✓ The act gave them ***freedom***. (noun)

11) He examined the document ***carefully***. (adverb)

- ✓ He examined the document with ***care***. (Noun with preposition)

12) We passed an ***anxious*** hour. (adjective)

- ✓ We passed an hour ***anxiously.*** (adverb)

13) Few write in a more ***interesting*** manner than him. (adjective)

- ✓ Few write more ***interestingly*** than him. (adverb)

14) He ***presumptuously*** ignored my advice. (adverb)

- ✓ He ***presumed*** to ignore my advice. (verb)

Replace the underlined Nouns by Verbs:

15) He rejected all our *proposals*.

- ✓ We ***proposed*** him all the times only to be rejected.

16) Steel gains *strength* from the addition of nickel.

- ✓ Steel ***strengthens*** by addition of nickel.

17) He made an *agreement* to supply me with firewood.

- ✓ He ***agreed*** to supply me firewood.

18) His *purpose* is not clear from his letter.

- ✓ He ***intends*** what is not clear from his letter.

19) You cannot gain *admission* without a ticket.

- ✓ You cannot be ***admitted*** without a ticket.
- ✓ We cannot a***dmit*** you without a ticket.

20) He has no *intention* of leaving the city. = He does not ***intend*** to leave the city.

21) I have a *disinclination* for work today. = I ***don't intend*** to work today.

22) He made a *success* of all his undertakings.

- ✓ He ***succeeded*** in all his undertakings.

23) These mangoes have a sweet *smell* but a sour taste.

- ✓ These mangoes ***smell*** sweet but have sour taste.

Replace the underlined Adverbs by Verbs:

24) The defenders *successfully* repelled every attack on the city.

- ✓ The defenders ***succeeded*** to repel every attack on the city.

25) This scene is *surpassingly* beautiful.

- ✓ This scene ***surpasses*** all in beauty.

26) He is *admittedly* the greatest general of the country.

- ✓ They ***admit*** him to be the greatest general of the country.

27) They welcomed the good news most _joyfully._
✓ They **_enjoyed_** very much to welcome the good news.

Replace the underlined Nouns & Adverbs by corresponding Adjectives:

28) In all _probability_ the day will be fine.
✓ It is all **_probable_** that the day will be fine.
29) The rats gave us a great deal of _trouble_.
✓ The rats were very **_troublesome_**.
30) He was dismissed for _negligence_ rather than _competence_.
✓ The office dismissed the **_negligent_** him rather than being less **_competent_**. / He was **_negligent,_** for this he was dismissed, but not for being less **_competent_**.
31) He was _admittedly_ clever, but he _evidently_ lacked industry.
✓ He was **_admitted_** (participle adj.) as clever, but it is **_evident_** he lacked industry.
32) The merchant had great _success_ in all his dealings, and was _naturally_ esteemed by his fellow citizens.
✓ The merchant was great **_successful_** in all his dealings, and it was **_natural_** his fellow citizens esteemed him.

Replace the underlined Verbs & Adjectives by corresponding Nouns:

33) Though the ant is small it is as _intelligent_ as the elephant.
✓ Though the ant is small, its **_intelligence_** is equal to an elephant.
34) He said he _regretted_ that he had _acted_ so hastily.
✓ He said that he is **_sorry_** for his **_act_** in hastiness.
35) He was so _active_ in his old age that everybody _admired_ him.
✓ The old man got **_admiration_** from everybody for his superb **_activeness_**.
36) Before I _pay_ you, what is _due_ you must _sign_ this receipt.
✓ I need your **_signature_** before the **_payment_** of the **_due_**.
37) The best way to be _healthy_ is to be _temperate_ in all things.
✓ No one can gain **_health_** without **_temperament_** in all things.

Replace the underlined Nouns & Adjectives by corresponding Adverbs:

38) Her dress was _poor_ and _mean_.
✓ She wore her dress **_poorly_** and **_meanly_**.

39) He broke the rules without any intention of doing so, but it does not follow that his punishment is *wrong*.

✓ He broke the rules without any intention of doing so, but it does not follow that he is punished ***wrongly***.

40) His mistake was *evident*, but his sincerity was also *obvious*.

✓ ***Evidently,*** he did mistake, but ***obviously*** he was sincere too.

41) By a *careful* analysis of these substances, you will see that they differ in *essence*.

✓ If you ***carefully*** analyze these substances ***essentially*** you will see the difference in them.

Conversion of Simple, Compound & Complex

78. In conversion, sl. No- 8. When we do transform Simple Sentences to Compound or Complex, simply we do change or enlarge —

- A participle or an adjective,
- A preposition with Noun or Gerund,
- An Infinitive verb,
- A Noun or the Phrase in apposition,
- The Absolute Phrase,
- Double Objects or A complement,
- The Adverb or Adverbial Phrases

— into Clauses (co-ordinate & sub-ordinate) accordingly; as,

By turn a participle into a clause

1) ***Having done*** his lesson, he went out to play cricket. (simple)

✓ *After he had done* his lesson, he went out to play cricket. (complex)

✓ *He had done* his lesson and then went out to play cricket. (compound)

Note: You may take a revision of the chapters— 'Classification of Sentences, based on structure', 'Analysis' & 'Synthesis' for better understand this part of conversion.

In conversion when we do convert a present participial into a clause, the clause may denote the following functions:

- Time,
- Cause,
- Concession,
- Condition, etc.

In the above sentence, 'Having done his lesson, he went out to play cricket', it denotes an action happened earlier than the other.

2) ***Walking*** *along the street* one day I saw a dead cobra.
 ✓ *While I was walking* along the street one day, I saw a dead cobra.
3) ***Being*** *overpowered*, he surrendered.
 ✓ *Because he was* overpowered, he surrendered.
4) ***Running*** *at top speed*, he got out of breath.
 ✓ *Because he ran* at top speed, he got out of breath.
5) ***Possessing*** *all the advantages of education and wealth*, he never made a name.
 ✓ *Although he possessed* all the advantages of education and wealth, he never made a name.
6) ***Following*** *my advice*, you will gain your object.
 ✓ *If you follow* my advice, you will gain your object.
7) Seven were killed, ***including the guard***.
 ✓ Seven were killed, *if the guard is included*.

And by Change of others:

8) To his eternal disgrace, he betrayed his country.
✓ He betrayed his country, and this was to his eternal disgrace. *(The relative phrase has turned into a clause)*
9) Besides robbing the pilgrims, he also murdered them.
✓ He not only robbed the pilgrims but also murdered them. *(The prepositional phrase has turned into a clause and that is linked with a co-ordinate conjunction with the main)*
10) He must work very hard to win the first prize.
✓ He must work very hard, or he will not win the first prize. *(The infinitive has turned into a clause)*
11) Notwithstanding his hard work, he didn't get the expected outcome.
✓ He worked hard, yet he did not get the expected outcome. *(The preposition with noun has turned into an independent clause)*
12) The teacher punished the boy for disobedience.
✓ The boy was disobedient, so the teacher punished him. *(The adverbial phrase has turned into a sub-ordinate adverbial clause)*
13) He finished his exercise and put away his books.
 ✓ Having finished his exercise, he put away his books.
 ✓ After he had finished his exercise, he put away his books.
14) Not only did his father give him money, but his mother did too.
 ✓ Besides his father giving him money, his mother also did the same.
 ✓ It is not that his father only gave him money but his mother too.
15) He was a mere boy but he offered to fight the giant.
 ✓ In spite of his being a mere boy, he offered to fight the giant.
 ✓ Though he was a mere boy, he offered to fight the giant.
16) He must not be late, or he will be punished.

✓ In the event of his being late, he will be punished.
✓ If he is late, he will be punished.

17) You must either pay the bill at once or return the goods.
✓ Falling prompt payment, the goods must be returned by you.
✓ If you not pay the bill at once, you must return the goods.

18) We must eat, or we cannot live.
✓ We eat to live. If we do not eat, we cannot live.

19) He confessed his crime.
✓ He confessed that he was guilty.
✓ He was guilty and he confessed it.

20) He bought his uncle's library.
✓ He bought the library which belonged to his uncle.
✓ He bought a library and it belonged to his uncle.

21) On the arrival of the mails the ship will leave.
✓ The ship will leave as soon as the mails arrive.
✓ The ship will leave after the mails arrive.

22) He owed his success to his father.
✓ It was owing to his father that he succeeded.
✓ He succeeded and this he owed to his father.

23) He worked hard to pass the examination.
✓ He worked hard so that he might pass the examination.
✓ He wanted to pass the examination and he worked hard for that reason.

24) Only Indians are admitted.
✓ If you are not an Indian you cannot be admitted.
✓ You are an Indian and you can be admitted.

25) He succeeded unexpectedly.
✓ He succeeded although his success was not expected.
✓ He succeeded and it was unexpected.

26) The management was thoroughly bad.
✓ The management was as bad as it could be.
✓ The management was bad and it was profoundly.

27) A man's modesty is in inverse proportion to his ignorance.
✓ The more ignorant a man is, the less modest he is.
✓ If the man is ignorant, he is less modest, is the correct proportion.

79. (From Complex to Simple)

How Noun Clauses turns to be Nouns or Noun phrase in the Simple Sentences:

28) He said <u>that he was innocent</u>. (Noun Clause)
✓ He declared **his innocence**. (Noun)

✓ He declared **to be innocent**. (adjective)

29) That you are drunk aggravates your offence.

✓ **Your drunkenness** aggravates your offence.

30) Tell me where you live.

✓ Tell me **your address**.

31) It is a pity that we should have to undergo this disgrace.

✓ *Our having to undergo this disgrace* is a pity.

32) ***It is proclaimed*** that all men found with arms will be shot.

✓ ***According to the proclamation*** all men found with arms will be shot. (by preposition with a noun)

33) He remarked how impudent the boy was.

✓ He remarked on the ***boy's impudence***. (by preposition with a noun)

34) How long I shall stay is doubtful.

✓ ***The duration of my stay*** is doubtful.

35) Except **that he hurt his hand**, he was lucky.

✓ Except ***for the hurt to his hand***, he was lucky.

By use of single adjective or adjective phrase for the Adjective Clauses:

36) He died in the village where he was born.

✓ He died in his **native** village.

37) The moment which is lost is lost forever.

✓ A lost moment is ***lost*** forever.

38) Men who have risen by their own exertions are always respected.

✓ ***Self-made*** men are always respected.

39) They that are whole have no need of the physician.

✓ ***Healthy persons*** have no need of the physician.

40) We came upon a hut where a peasant lived.

✓ We came upon a ***peasant's hut***.

41) Youth is the time when the seeds of character are sown.

✓ Youth is the ***time for the formation of character***.

42) The exact time when this occurred has not been ascertained.

✓ The exact time ***of the occurrence*** has not been ascertained.

43) The son who was his chief pride in his old age is dead.

✓ His son, ***the pride of his old age***, is dead.

44) I have no advice that I can offer you.

✓ I have no advice ***to offer*** you.

Study how the Adverb Clauses turn to adverbs or adverbial phrases mostly, and the sentences become Simple Sentences:

45) The captain was annoyed that we had not carried out his orders.
✓ The captain was annoyed **at our not having carried out his orders**. (why was the captain annoyed at?)
46) You can talk as much as you like.
✓ You can talk **to your heart's content**. (how much can I talk?)
47) Success & everything come if a man will only work & wait.
✓ Only work and waiting **diligently** bring success and everything to a man. (how?)
48) I am pushing my business wherever I can find an opening.
✓ I am pushing my business **in every possible direction**. (where?)
49) He will not pay unless he is compelled.
✓ He will pay **only under compulsion**. (in what condition?)
50) You have succeeded better than you hoped.
✓ You have succeeded **beyond your hopes**.
51) When the cat is away the mice will play.
✓ **In the absence of the cat** the mice will play.
52) He does not always speak as he thinks.
✓ He does not always speak **his thoughts**.
53) He was so tired that he could not stand.
✓ He was **too tired to** stand.
54) A soldier will always do as he is commanded by his superiors.
✓ A soldier will always carry out (or execute) the **commands of his superiors**. (noun phrase)
55) I was surprised when I heard him talk so.
✓ I was **surprised to hear** him talk so.
56) If I make a promise, I keep it.
✓ I make promise **only to keep** it.
57) As the war ended, the soldiers returned.
✓ The war **being ended**, the soldiers returned. (turns to present participle)
58) While there is life there is hope.
✓ Life and hope are **inseparable**. (use of an adjective, in place of adverb of condition)
59) As you sow, so you will reap.
✓ You will but reap the fruits of your sowing. (turns to a gerund)

Conversion of Compound to Complex

60) Search his pockets and you will find the watch.
✓ If you search his pockets, you will find the watch.

61) Do as I tell you, or you will regret it.
✓ Unless you do as I tell you, you will regret it.
62) Waste not, want not.
✓ If you do not waste, you will not want.
63) He wishes to become learned; therefore, he is studying hard.
✓ He is studying hard so that he may become learned.
64) I am glad that he has recovered from illness.
✓ He has recovered from illness and I am glad at it.
65) We can prove that the earth is round.
✓ The earth is round, and we can prove it.
66) I have found the book that I had lost.
✓ I had lost a book, but I have found it.
67) If he is at home, I shall see him.
✓ He may be at home, and in that case, I shall see him.
68) We sow so that we may reap.
✓ We desire to reap; therefore, we sow.

Conversion of Narration

80. Conversion of Narration (Indirect to Direct & vice-versa; Sl. No-9): For more, go through the chapter of Narration Change, i.e., only to the previous chapter. Here is provided a space not more than a little much:

1) He enquired whether my name was Peter.
✓ He said to me, "Is not your name, Peter?"
2) As the stranger entered the town, he met by a policeman who asked him if he was a traveler. He replied carelessly that it would appear so.
✓ As the stranger entered the town, a policeman met him who asked, "Are you a traveler?" "So, it would appear", he answered carelessly.
3) The prince said that it gave him great pleasure to be there that evening.
✓ The prince said, "It gives me great pleasure to be here this evening."
4) He said, "Let us wait for the award."
✓ He proposed that they should wait for the award.
5) The teacher often says to me, "If you don't work hard, you will fail."
✓ The teacher often says if I don't work hard, I shall fail.

Conversion: From One to Thirty-Two

81. For conversion one sentence to thirty-two, we choose here 'a simple sentence' which is also an Assertive Affirmative, in the Active Voice; it is also in the Present Indefinite Tense and of Direct Speech, besides being a_Simple sentence. We can convert the simple sentence to as many. Read the sentence:

'You do the work.'

Type of Sentences	Examples
1. Assertive & Affirmative	You do the work.
1. Assertive & Negative	You don't do the work.
2. Interrogative	Do you do the work?
3. Imperative	Do the work. / I let you to do the work. You are ordered/ advised to do the work. You are asked to do the work.
4. Optative	Let you do the work. / I wish you to do the work. /May God give you power to do the work.
5. Exclamatory	What! you have not yet done the work.
6. Complex	What you do is a work.
7. Compound	Someone will do the work and it is you.
8. Passive	The work is done by you.
9. Indirect speech	He asks me to do the work.
10. Present Continuous	You are doing the work.
11.Present Perfect	You have done the work.
12.Present Perfect Continuous	You have been doing the work since Friday.
13.Past Indefinite	You did the work.

14. Past Continuous	You were doing the work
15. Past Perfect	You had done the work.
16. Past Perfect Continuous	You had been doing the work for three hours.
17. Future Indefinite	You will do the work
18. Future Continuous	You will be doing the work.
19. Future Perfect	You will have done the work.
20. Future Perfect Continuous	You will have been doing the work before we reach there.

Type of Sentences: now by modals	**Examples**
21. By use of **'can'**	You can do the work. — express ability
22. By use of **'may'**	You may do the work. — giving permission
23. By use of **'must'**	You must do the work. — strong necessity
24. By use of **'will'**	You will do the work. — futurity
25. By use of **'could'**	You could do the work. — past ability
26. By use of **'might'**	You might do the work. — past possibility
27. By use of **'should'**	You should the work. — morality
28. By use of **'would'**	You would do the work. — futurity in past
29. By use of **'ought to'**	You ought to do the work. — obligatory
30. By use of **'used to'**	You used to do the work. — past habit

31. By use of **'need'** You need to do the work. — necessity

32. By use of **'dare'** How dare you to do the work! — wonder at courage

9. The Use of Punctuations (includes 16)

82. **What is Punctuation?** = Punctuation is an art of giving the expression a pause by some marks or points (not dividing a sentence), so as to make the meaning clearer.

Let's see the punctuations at a glance:

Sl. No	***Punctuations***	***Signs***	***Representing or Meanings (main)***
(1)	Capital Letters	**A, B, C ... Z**	To begin a sentence or fresh line of poetry
(2)	Full Stop	**(.)**	Greatest pause, or end of an Assert. or Imperative Sentence
(3)	Question Mark	**(?)**	Is used after each Direct Question.
(4)	Exclamation	**(!)**	Used after Interjections or after Exclaim. Sentence
(5)	Comma	**(,)**	Shortest pause, after Nominative Absolute, etc.
(6)	Semicolon	**(;)**	A pause of greater importance than comma
(7)	Colon	**(:)**	Introducing a quotation
(8)	Dash	**(—)**	To indicate an abrupt stop, or change of thought.
(9)	Hyphen	**(-)**	used to connect the parts of a Compound word
(10)	Apostrophe	**(...')**	Show omission of letter(s), genitive case

(11)	Inverted Commas	('…'/ "…")	To enclose words of the speaker
(12) *(13)* *(14)* *(15)*	Use of Brackets Asterisk (*), Dot-dot-dot …, Oblique (/)	(…),{…}, […]	*To enclose a parenthesis* To point out something is missing To show incomplete statement: To mean 'either'/ 'or'
(16)	Parenthesis	point out by (…)/ ,…,	an inserted extra statement by a word, phrase or a clause, used separately in the sentence.

Read them again with examples. Let's begin with the use of Capital Letter.

Use of Capital Letters

1. Use of Capital Letters

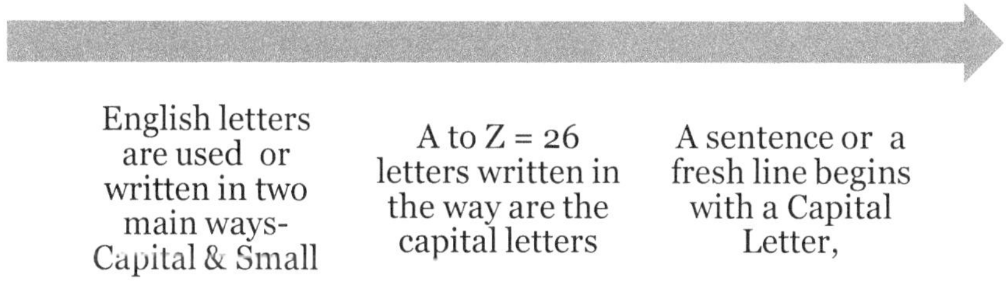

English letters are used or written in two main ways- Capital & Small

A to Z = 26 letters written in the way are the capital letters

A sentence or a fresh line begins with a Capital Letter,

Sl. No	Illustration	Examples
1.	First letter of a sentence must be in capital letter.	• ***He*** was a great ruler of ***Maura*** dynasty in ***India***.
2.	First letter of Proper Noun or Proper adjective must be in capital.	• ***Gautama Buddha*** never met with ***Asoka***. You must love an ***Indian***.
3.	The title of an Honorable person must be in capital.	• ***The Minister*** met with the ***Principal*** of the college.
4.	First letter of a poetic line (each) must be in capital.	• ***Twinkle Twinkle*** little star, • ***How*** I wonder what you are.

5.	'I' to mean first person and 'God' to mean almighty, & all Nouns & Pronouns which indicate the Deity, always be in Capital Letter.	• With due respect, ***I*** like to draw your attention. He prayed to ***God*** whole night. The ***Lord***, He is the ***God***.
6.	'O' of interjection must be in capital.	• ***Oh*** my ***God***! he is no more.
7.	First letter of a quotation must be in capital.	• He said, "***Will*** you lend me your book, please?"
8.	Abbreviation is written in capital after use of full stop.	• ***L.L.B., M.A., B.A., B.Sc., M.K. Gandhi was*** the father of nation.

2. **Full Stop,**
3. **Question &**
4. **Exclamation**

2. Full Stop (.)	**Examples**
a) After each complete sentence	• A farmer had three sons. Come here.
b) After short forms or abbreviations	5 a.m., M.Phil., Mr. P.N. Sarkar, Saidpur B.M.A. High School.
3. Question Mark (?)	**Examples**
a) After a direct question	• What's your name? • How old are you?
But not after an indirect question	• He asked me what my name was.
4. Exclamation Mark (!)	**Examples**
a) After any expression of emotion as, wonder, fear, excitement, joy etc.	• What a beautiful sight! / How strange! • Hurrah! We have won the match.
b) After interjections or any part of speech used so:	• Milton! Thou shouldst be living at this hour. Gone! Dead! Accident!

- Oh! Hurrah! Alas! Oh dear! etc.

5. Comma (,)

> The comma represents the shortest pause and is the most frequently used sign of all marks.

Study the uses of Comma (,) in the following chart:

5. Comma (,)	**Examples**
a) Between words of same parts of speech or **repeated words**, if used in a sequence.	• **Pompi, Pieu,** & **Jhumpa** are her friends. • He **went**, **found, chose,** & **bought** the things. • She is **long**, **fair, laughing,** & **kind-hearted**. • I will **never, never** go there. • You **must, must** do it.
b) Between phrases, clauses of same character, often to avoid the repetition of subject. **Exceptions:** But when only two words or phrases of the same character are joined by '**and**', the comma is not required.	• I went to Kolkata, met my aunt, & came back. • He entered the room, wrote a letter, and then left the place. • Ram and Shyam went there. • Swimming in the river and swimming in the pond are good for health.
c) But when words go in pairs, the comma is placed between each pair.	• Rifles and bayonets, spades and axes, drums and trumpets littered the ground.
d) Between co-ordinate clauses. (We may not use too.)	• He is ill, and his father too is away. • He is away now, but will return shortly.

e) To mark off noun or noun clauses from adjective clauses, if there is more than one.	• I do not know where he is, when he will come, or what his present state is. • I know the girl who is beautiful, who is fair, who is soft-hearted, and who is proud.
Exceptions: i) When there is only one adjective clause, it does not need to separate from its noun.	• The dog I bought has died. • I saw your brother who told me this. • I saw your brother, who told me this. (exception)
ii) But if that is lengthy, comma can be used.	• The man, who promised to help me if I would approach him, has gone away.
iii) It is applicable even to a long complex noun clause, used as a subject.	• That his brother who has done so much for the club will be elected its secretary, is known to all.
f) <u>To mark off adverbial clauses or phrases in apposition or the Absolute Phrases</u>, & also participial phrases that might be expanded into clauses or sentences.	• In order that you may succeed, I shall help you with money. • Saral, after he had left the place, went direct to the Magistrate. • Ram, having returned home, went to see her. • Disappointed of the prize, he left the place.
g) Comma is used even to mark off a single adverb in a sentence.	• This, then, is my story. • I shall, however, help you.
Exception: But when the Adverbial clause or the phrase follows the principal clause, the comma is omitted.	• I was glad when I saw you. • He came after I had left.
h) Before or after the **Vocative Case** or the **Nominative of Address**.	• Tarun, come here. / Stop, boys. • Sir, be seated, please. • Hello, who is speaking?
i) <u>Before & after the phrase in apposition</u>. *If ends with it, use full stop.*	• Ashoka, the emperor of India, took Buddhism. He came, to the surprise of all. • A tiger, two meters long, was shot dead.

j) After an **absolute construction**:	• The sun having set, we left the place. • Dinner over, the guests departed. • To tell you the truth, I consider him fool.
k) After words like 'yes', 'no':	• Has he come? No, he hasn't. • Will you go to school? Yes, I'll.
l) To separate the name of a town, a state, a country in the same sentence (to indicate the omission of a preposition)	• He is from Kolkata, West Bengal, India. • (He is from Kolkata of West Bengal in India.)
m) To separate the day of a month from its year. (Here also to indicate the omission of a preposition)	• She was born on 8th May, 2002. • (She was born on 8th May of the year 2002.)
n) To indicate the omission of a verb	• Virtue leads to happiness; vice, to misery. (Vice leads to misery.)
o) To mark off a quotation.	• He said, "I love you."

6. Semicolon (;) &
7. Colon (:)

The semicolon (;) denotes a longer pause than the comma. In other words, it represents a pause of greater importance than that of comma.

The colon (:) introduces a quotation or examples, often followed by a dash.

The Use of Semicolon (;)

Semicolon (;)	Examples
a) Between co-ordinate clauses when are not joined by conjunctions.	○ To err is human; to forgive, divine. ○ I have heard his statement; it is improbable story.

b) When they are joined by conjunctions that express **contrast** or **inference** like— **therefore**, **yet**, **then**, **however**, **so**, **otherwise** – they follow semicolon, and after them, we use generally a comma (,), except 'yet' & 'then' (they are not followed by comma.)

- He is ill***; therefore,*** he will not come.
- He helped me to his best***; yet*** I failed in my attempt.
- You don't believe me***; then*** I am leaving the job.
- She was weak student***; however,*** she passed.
- He did not work hard***; so,*** he could not succeed.
- You must do it for him***; otherwise,*** he will be angry with us.

c) When commas are used in smaller division, the semicolon can be used there in some larger division, even before a conjunction.

- The boy, who had stood first in the examination, was given a very good prize**;** and it was expected, this would encourage him to exert himself still more to keep up his position.
- He was a brave, large-hearted man**;** and we all honored him.

The Use of Colon (:)

Colon (:)	Examples
a) After a statement, **complete in itself**; when followed by another or a series, connected without a **conjunction**, or a **dash** or a full **stop**; may refer cause, result or contrast.	○ He is from Kolkata, West Bengal, India**:** he worked his best and won the silver cup. ○ He stood first**:** I stood last. ○ They were without provision**:** they suffered a good deal.
b) Before **giving some examples**	○ Examples of common gender are**:** parent, sovereign, child, etc. ○ Send me the following goods**:** a good pen, some paper, one knife.
Can be replaced by a dash (—)	○ She wanted— a good pen, some paper, one knife, etc.
c) To introduce a quotation:	○ She said**:** Of all my friends, you are the best.
Can be replaced by a dash (—), or *comma + inverted commas*	○ She said— Of all my friends, you are the best.

- She said, "Of all my friends, you are the best."

8. Use of Dash (—)

Dash (—)	Examples
a) To mark an abrupt break or stop or change of thought, in the sentence	1) We were all guilty of this, I, he and — . 2) Here is a great—scholar all of us.
b) To mark 'words in apposition' as explanation or examples; or 'to resume a scattered subject:	1) I have lost my all—health, wealth & reputation. 2) Raima, Kabita, Sabita—all were present there. 3) Friends, companies, relatives—all deserted him.
c) To give examples:	Verbs are two kinds—Finite & Non-finite.
d) To insert a parenthesis (a comment made aside or as addition) as b)	1) He told us—and he wept as he did so—how he had lost his all. 2) At the age of five—such is the power of genius—he could read English quite well.
e) To introduce quotation,	She said— Of all my friends, you are the best.
f) To indicate hesitation.	I am un—able. / I have fai—led.

9. Use of Hyphen (-) & 10. Apostrophe (')

Hyphen (-)	Examples
a) to form compound words,	Father-in-law / son-in-law; passer-by, man-of-war, jack-of-all-trades, etc.
b) to carry out words from one line to another.	He has no abi- -lity.

Apostrophe (-')	Examples
a) **In contracted forms** as showed in verbs: to indicate some letter or letters have been left out & to show time)	I'm, you're, (s)he's, they're, e'en (for even), hon'ble (for honorable), etc. I get up early at 4 o'clock in the morning.

b) To indicate **the genitive case** of nouns & certain pronouns. (See noun's chapter for details of Genitive case)	It is Rahim's book. The table's legs are broken. God's mercy etc.
c) To ***form the plural of letters & figures***	Underline your i's, and cross your t's. Add two 5's & four 2's.

11. Inverted Commas

Double Inverted Comma ("-")	**Examples**
a) To quote somebody's speech	"Where are you going?", asked his mother.
b) To mention 'a title of a work' or 'a book'; & also to point out some particular word, phrase or a clause.	o He wrote **"Pather Panchali"**, **"Apur Sansar"** etc. o Here **"me"** refers to the poet. o The word **"right"** is an adjective here.
Single Inverted Comma ('-')	Examples
a) To introduce a quotation within another quotation.	The teacher says to the boys, "Never say, **'I can't'**."
b) Do all the functions of the Double Inverted Comma:	He wrote 'Pather Panchali', 'Apur Sansar' etc. Here 'me' refers to the poet. The word 'right' is a verb here.

Brackets, Asterisk, Dot-dot-dot & Oblique

12. Use of Brackets (...), {...}, [...];
13. Asterisk (*);
14. Dot-dot-dot (...), &
15. Oblique (/)

Brackets ( )/ { }/ [ ]	**Examples**
a) *To enclose a parenthesis* like a pair of dashes or commas. **Note:** When we need more than a pair of brackets, generally we use the others	• He learnt (such is the power of genius) the alphabet in one day. • He learnt— such is the power of genius— the alphabet in one day.

for almost same purpose or meanings.	• He learnt, such is the power of genius, the alphabet in one day.
b) To introduce an explanation (as done by dash)	• I have lost all I had in the bag (five rupees). • I have lost all I had in the bag—five rupees.
Asterisk(s) (*)	**Examples**
a) To point out something is missing or intentionally left out (words or clauses)	My brother * * at last succeeded in getting the post. (* *who had tried so long)
b) To show importance or note of something.	* It was very praiseworthy. / ** it is a verb.
Dot-dot-dot (...)	**Examples**
a) To show incomplete statement:	He did, because ...
Oblique (/)	**Examples**
a) To mean 'either'/ 'or'	He / She is responsible. (He **or** She is responsible)

Parenthesis

16. Parenthesis

What is Parenthesis?

- **A word**, **phrase, clause** or a **sentence** when inserted as an extra explanation or idea into a large sentence or passage & which would be complete without it & generally which is marked off or separated from the rest mainly by brackets or dashes or commas, before & after of a parenthesis.
  - A parenthetic phrase or clause ***do function*** as the ***'case in apposition'*** in a sentence. But *when a parenthesis gives explanation* a '*phrase in apposition' adds information*.

Examples of Parenthesis (Phrase, Clause or Sentence):

1) He is, ***to tell the truth***, not quite frank.

2) I was, ***to be frank***, much surprised of her come.
3) I am, ***of me***, ok.
4) The sun is, ***so to speak***, the lamp of the universe.
5) This is, ***I think***, a bare truth.
6) The sun is, ***so to speak***, the source of all energy on earth.
7) If you are in the wrong *(**and I am sure you are, whatever you may say**)* why don't you admit it?

➢ In above all cases the '**phrases within commas before & after**', can be analyzed separately and similarly can be taken out without injuring the sense.

1) He is, **I am sure**, something like a poet.
2) His conduct, **I believe**, is good.
3) Why do you, my friend, **I don't know**, hate me?
4) Why do you, **it is not clear**, not talk to me now-a-days?
5) But you should, **I am likely agreed**, do so.

➢ All the above are simple sentences while the **bold written words are parenthetic expressions**, they are thrown into the main sentence, like a phrase in apposition or an Absolute Phrase. They can be analyzed separately. In the sentences they **are thrown in as independent elements**; and they may be taken out without injuring the sentences.

'Parenthetic' expressions in compound

1) He is, **I am sure**, something of a poet & his poetry are too good to read by others.
2) His conduct, **I believe**, is good & too good to converse with.
3) Why do you, my friend, **I don't know**, give me light and snatch it away?
4) Why do you, it **is not clear**, begin to talk and stop forever?

➢ All the above are compound sentences with two principals while the **bold written words are parenthetic expressions**; they can be analyzed separately. In the sentences they **are thrown in as independent elements**; and they may be taken out without injuring the sense of the sentences.

'Parenthetic' expressions in complex

1) He is, **I am sure**, something of a poet who reads alone his poetry.
2) His conduct, **I believe**, is what is not suitable for his own age.
3) He is the man who, **I believe**, did it.
4) This is the boy who, **I think**, came the other day.

- All the above are complex sentences with only one principal & one sub-ordinate clauses while the **bold written words are parenthetic expressions**; they can be analyzed separately.

Note: The ***double commas***, ***dashes*** or ***brackets*** are generally used for such Parenthetic Expressions.

10. Subject & Verb Agreement

83. Actually, there should not be at all such a chapter to call, '**subject-verb agreement**'; for such thing does not refer to any new thing, or any essence to discuss separately from others. However, looking at the importance and need for different competitive examinations, here it is made a sum up or summary of all, related verb and subject relation, or so called the conjugation of subjects and verbs; (i.e., different verb forms relating person, number (of the subjects), change of verb forms as per tense, voice change, narration change, assertive, interrogative, affirmative, negative, use of different moods, and words, and whatever it can include thus. However, who already gets mastery over English Grammar can go through the chapter considering it as a revision of their lesion they have already learnt.

    Sometimes to brief the discussion, as it tends to be long, I have freely chosen multi charts to give focus on the forms of verbs according to subjects, and somewhere with examples. A learner's task is to go through all of them giving equal importance to each point, and discussion.

    Let's begin—

84. **Read the sentences: Underline the subject and the verb in each sentence:**

    India's ambassador to United Nations, **TS Tirumurti** on Sunday (local time) **expressed** grief over the sudden death of India's Representative at Ramallah, Mukul Arya.

Mukul Arya was found dead inside the Indian embassy in Palestine on Sunday. "**This is** truly shocking. A wonderful **colleague snatched** away so young. My deepest condolences to his family," **Tirumurti tweeted**.

(Have you noticed in the sentence the verbs always have agree in number, person and tense of the sentence. This is called the subject & verb agreement.)

Study each chart with equal importance

1. 'Be' Verbs:

Tenses	Persons	Singular	Plural
Present Tense >am, is, are 1/1/4	1st Person	I am	We are
	2nd Person	You are	You are
	3rd Person	S/he is	They are
Past Tense >was, were 2/4	1st Person	I was	We were
	2nd Person	You were	You were
	3rd Person	S/he was	They were
Future Tense >shall be, will be 2/4	1st Person	I **shall be**	We **shall be**
	2nd Person	You will be	You will be
	3rd Person	S/he will be	They will be

2. 'Have' Verbs:

Tenses	Persons	Singular	Plural
Present Tense >has, have 1/5	1st Person	I have	We have
	2nd Person	You have	You have

	3rd Person	S/he has	They have
Past Tense **>had** **6 of 6**	1st Person	I had	We had
	2nd Person	You had	You had
	3rd Person	S/he had	They had
Future Tense **>shall have, will have** **2/4**	1st Person	**I shall have**	**We shall have**
	2nd Person	You will have	You will have
	3rd Person	S/he will have	They will have

3. 'Do' Verbs & Others in Simple Tenses

Tenses	Persons	Singular	Plural
Present Simple **> do, does** **1/5**	1st Person	I do	We do
	2nd Person	You do	You do
	3rd Person	S/he does	They do
Past Simple **>did** **6 of 6**	1st Person	I did	We did
	2nd Person	You did	You did
	3rd Person	S/he did	They did
Future Simple **>shall do, will do** **2/4**	1st Person	**I shall do**	**We shall do**
	2nd Person	You will do	You will do
	3rd Person	S/he will do	They will do

4. 'Do' Verbs & Others in Continuous Tenses

Tenses	**Persons**	**Singular**	**Plural**
Present Continuous with **'be'** helping verb >am/is/are **doing** **1/1/4**	1st Person	**I am doing**	We are doing
	2nd Person	You are doing	You are doing
	3rd Person	**S/he is doing**	They are doing
Past Continuous **>was/were doing** **2/4**	1st Person	I was doing	We were doing
	2nd Person	You were doing	You were doing
	3rd Person	S/he was doing	They were doing
Future Continuous **>shall/will be doing** **2/4**	1st Person	**I shall be doing**	**We shall be doing**
	2nd Person	You will be doing	You will be doing
	3rd Person	S/he will be doing	They will be doing

5. 'Do' Verbs & Others in Perfect Tenses

Tenses	**Persons**	**Singular**	**Plural**
Present Perfect: >has/have +p.p. of base verb (done) **1/5**	1st Person	I have done	We have done
	2nd Person	You have done	You have done
	3rd Person	**S/he has done**	They have done
	1st Person	I had done	We had done

Past Perfect >had done 6 of 6	2nd Person	You had done	You had done
	3rd Person	S/he had done	They had done
Future Perfect >shall/will have done 2/4	1st Person	I shall have done	We shall have done
	2nd Person	You will have done	You will have done
	3rd Person	She will have done	They will have done

6. 'Do' Verbs & Others in Perfect Continuous Tenses

Tenses	Persons	Singular	Plural
Present Perfect Continuous with '**have**' + '**been**' & **continuous form of verb** >has/have been doing -1/5	1st Person	I have been doing	We have been doing
	2nd Person	You have been doing	You have been doing
	3rd Person	S/he has been doing	They have been doing
Past Perfect Continuous >had been doing 6 of 6	1st Person	I had been doing	We had been doing
	2nd Person	You had been doing	You had been doing
	3rd Person	S/he had been doing	They had been doing
Future Perfect Continuous	1st Person	I shall have been doing	We shall have been doing
	2nd Person	You will have been doing	You will have been doing

>shall/will have been doing 2/4	3rd Person	She will have been doing	They will have been doing

85. The following subjects in bold letters are followed by Singular Verbs:

(1) An **Uncountable Noun** always follows a verb of Third Person Singular Number.

- **Water** is essential for us.
- **The grass** was getting long.
- **The boy's hair** will be cut etc.

(2) **'Much', 'little', 'a little',** and **'the little' are used with uncountable nouns, and they take** always the singular verb in a sentence; as,

- **Much** money has been spent trying to repair the fan.
- **Only a little** of the food has been eaten.
- **The little food** we had was eaten up by a cat.
- **Little sugar** is left with us.

(3) A word or phrase of **measurement** takes a singular verb of 3rd person.

- **Five miles** *is* too far to walk.
- **One hundred rupees** *is* to cover.
- **Two hours** *is* a long time to wait.
- **Two hundred rupees** *seems* reasonable for the article.

(4) When the subject phrase begins with **'The number of/A large amount of'/ 'One of',** the verb is singular.

- **The number of months** in a year *is* twelve.
- **The number of problems** we face *is* increasing.
- **The number of messages** I got *was* increasing from her.
- **A large amount of money** *was* collected by Sarada.
- **A large amount of people** *gathers* in a fair.
- **One of** you *is* responsible for the sin/crime/murder.
- **The number of students** in the class *is* fifty.

(5) **'Someone/*No one/None/ Nothing'** or **None of/ Neither of/ Either of/Any of + plural noun'** follows singular verb.

- **Someone/No one/None** *comes*

- here.
- **Nothing** *comes out* of nothing.
- **None of** these pens *works.*
- **Neither of** my friends *speaks* French.
- **Either of** these watches *is* stolen.
- If **any of** your friends *is* interested, let me know.

(6) When the two words or phrases **express a single thing** or **a unit**, the verb must be singular.

- **Rice and fish** *is* main food of Bengali people.
- **Law and order** *was* under control.
- **Time and tides** *waits* for none

(7) **Titles** and **names** of a country, book, organization or a state, may look plural in form, but they always take a singular verb; as they refer to one thing; as,

- **The Beijing Olympics** *was* held in 2008.
- **The United States of America** *is* a country to the north-west of India.
- **The United Nations** *is* the name of an organization.
- '**Love and Reason**' *is* a collection of poems.
- '**The Three Musketeers**' *is* a classic creation of the author.

(8) When two singular nouns are joined by '**and**', they make plural number, but if the both names or nouns refer to **single person**, singular verb is to be used or followed; as,

- **The Headmaster** and **Goutam Das** *is* one person.
- **Peter** & **Mr. Peter** *is* only one person.
- **The secretary** and **chairman** of the school *comes* to the institution this morning.

But, if they refer two different persons, joined by '**and**', they are always followed by plural verb; as,

- **The Secretary** and **Goutam Das** *are* present there in the meeting hall.
- **Saint Peter** & **Mr. Peter** *were* two different men.
- **The secretary** and the **chairman** of the school *were* there in the meeting hall.

86. In the following case the verb agrees either Singular or Plural, it depends on sense.

(9) A verb, agrees singular or plural, according to the sense, with the words– '**Who** or **What**', **What/Which** + **Noun**' etc.

- **Who** *knows* the man? /**Who** *are* the people behind the main door?
- **What** *has* happened? /**What** numbers *is* **he** talking about? /**What** numbers *are* **you** talking about?
- **What/Which day** *is* suitable?
- **What/Which days** *are* suitable?
- **What numbers** *are* shown in the result board?

(10) **If two** or **more singular subjects** are preceded by **Each/Every/No** and even joined by 'and' the verb is singular.

- **Each boy** and **each girl** *was* given a sweet.
- **Every teacher** and **every student** *has* to have an identity card.
- **Every man**, **woman** and **child** *was* going to fair.
- **No boarder** and **no caretaker** *was* found in the hostel.

(11)But if '**each**'/**every** follows a plural subject, the verb is plural.

- The pupils **each** *have* to give the test.
- The customers **each** *have* to pass through the gate.
- People **every one** there *were* involved in the riot.

(12) Adjective '**No**' is generally followed by a singular subject or noun, and thus, a singular verb is used. But, it is followed by plural Nouns, the plural verb form is used.

- **No pupil** *has* failed in the examination.
- **No pupils** *have* passed the examination.

(13) After '**There**' the verb agrees with its complements.

- There *was* **a loud bang**.
- There *were* **some books** on the table.

(14) Some **nouns with plural look**, take singular verb.

- **The news** *is* very good. **Mumps** *is* a dangerous disease. **Gymnastics** *is* a physical exercise. **Physics** *is* a subject. **The innings** *is* well played.

(15) Some **nouns, always in plural form,** also take plural verb.

- My few **belongings** *have* been packed. The paper **goods** *are* cheap. My **savings** *have* been gone to buy a car.
- The **earnings** of the family *are* poor. (however, it means the earnings come from different sources or from more than one member of the family.)

(16) **After a fraction** the verb agrees with the **following noun**.

- **Three quarters** of a **potato** *is* water.
- **Almost half** the **plants** *were* dead.

(17) When the subject denotes **amount**, the verbs agree with the subject in number and person.

- **A large amount of money** *was* collected by Sarada.
- **Large amounts of money** *were* collected (for different schemes.)

(18) If a phrase comes after the noun, the verb agrees according to first noun.

- **The house** between the two gardens *is* empty.
- **The houses** between the two roads *have* been burnt.
- **The price** of books *has* gone up.
- **The price** of daily commodities *is* going up.
- **The cover pages** of his creation *are* not bad.
- **The condition** of the patients *was* not out of danger.
- **The color** of those flowers *is* attractive.
- **The colors** you chose *were* excellent.

(19) A phrase in apposition does not make the subject plural; here too, the verb follows the first noun.

- ***Mr. Das*, the headmaster**, *is* an honorable person.
- ***My colleagues*, the teachers of B.M.A. High School**, *are* honest.

(20) A phrase with '**as well as**', '**along with**', **together with**, **accompanied with**, '**with**', '**of**' does not make the subject plural; verb here simply follow the 1st noun/pronoun

- ***Mr. Sarkar* as well as** his brothers *was* in the train.
- ***The headmaster* along with** all his teachers *was* honored.
- ***The students*, together with** their English teacher, *have* performed the drama.
- ***Mr. Sarkar* accompanied by** his family members *is* attending the ceremony.
- ***The tigress* with** its cubs *is* playing.
- ***This pair* of** trousers *needs* cleaning.

(21) After '**not only...but also**', the verb agrees with the nearest phrase

- **Not only** Ashok **but also** his friends *are* purchasing the book.
- **Not only** the players **but also** the coach *was* given warm welcome.

(22) When two phrases are joined by '**Either…or**', '**or**', '**Neither…nor**', the verb usually agrees with the nearest

- **Either** Saturday **or** Sunday *is* OK.
- **Either** my brother **or** my sisters *are* looking after the pet.
- **Ajanta** or **you** *are* to blame.
- **Neither** you **nor** he *is* reliable.
- **Neither** Raju **nor** his sisters *have* come.

(23) '**Some**' refers to **both singular** and **plural**.

- **Some people** *were* there till then.
- **Some** *hears* the voice and runs towards the spot.

(24) Two or more words or phrases when connected by '**and**' or such conjunctions, the verb will be plural; but when they refer to **same person/idea** the verb will be singular.

- **You, he and I** *are* very sorry. / **I, he and you** *were* guilty.
- **Swapan** and **Goutam** *go* travelling at weekends.
- **Rice and wheat** *are* imported. (Separately they are meant)
- **Rice and wheat** *is* my food of the evening. (Referring a 'meal')
- **The H.M. of the school** and **Goutam babu** *is* the same person.
- **The Headmaster** and **Secretary of the Institution** *is* one.
- **The Headmaster** and the **Secretary of the Institution** *are* against this proposal.

(25) When a subject follows '**Most of**', '**A number of**', '**The majority of**', '**A lot of**' – a plural verb is generally used.

- **Most of patients** *were* released.
- **A number of people** *have* applied for the post.
- **A majority of members** *were* opposed to the policy.
- **A lot of people** *are* facing the problem.

(26) But the subject begins with '**The number of**' always follow a singular verb and '**The numbers**' follow a plural verb.

- **The number of people** *has* increased suddenly.
- **The numbers** you have mentioned *were* fake.

(27) '**Many a/many an**' agrees singular verb

- **Many a** man *has* been invited in the meeting.
- **Many an** admirer *has* praised his paintings.

(28) **'a great many/too many'** agrees plural verb

- **A great many** children *are* making much noise.
- **Too many** mistakes *have* been made in this writing.

87. When Noun Agrees Plural Verb:

(29) **'many', 'a few'** –are used with countable nouns, and they take the plural verb in a sentence; as,

- Many of my friends *are* waiting for their results.
- A few of my colleagues *are* rich ones.

(30) A **pair noun** is plural in form and takes a plural verb.

- His new **glasses** *are* very fine.
- My **trousers** *are* grey in color.
- **Scissors** *are* used for cutting papers.

(31) But if such noun is used with a phrase preceding it, the verb follows the first noun.

- This pair of **trousers** *needs* cleaning.
- Two pairs of **trousers** *are* needed.

(32) **Group or collective nouns** (when they are meant individually or different opinions are hint) often follow plural verbs

- My **family** *have* not come to decisive position to move to Siliguri.
- The **crowd** *were* in a happy mood. They were shouting, dancing, etc.
- The **team** *are* not playing well this season.
- **The group members** *have been* debating which song to sing.
- **The jury members** *were* different in opinions.

(33) But **when it refers to impersonal unit**, **same thought**, or **express single idea**, the verb is singular.

- The **family** *owns* a car. The **team** *is* full of energy.
- The **govt.** *is* considering the tax problem.
- The **whole class** *was* told to stand up.
- The **committee** *needs* more time.
- The **group** *sings* really well.
- The **jury** *takes* the right decision.

(34) **When we talk about whole group**, we use singular verb. But **when we talk of people's thoughts**, it agrees plural verb.

- **The committee** *consists of* ten members.
- **The committee** *don't* understand what the expert is saying.

(35) '**More than one**' agrees with singular verb but '**more than two**' take a plural verb.

- **More than one bridge** *has* been damaged.
- **More than two bridges** *have* been damaged.

(36) The nouns e.g., **police**, **people**, **livestock**, **cattle**, **poultry**, **dozen** etc. have a plural meaning agree with plural verbs.

- **The police** *arrest* a man for questioning.
- **People** *have* to follow the rules of the country.
- **Cattle** *are* kept in a farm for their milk and meat.
- **A dozen of pencils** *cost of* rupees fifteen.

(37) **Certain adjectives preceded by the definite article** are used as nouns, they talk of groups of people and they take plural verb.

- **The blind** *are* not neglected nowadays.
- **The rich** *are* not always happy.
- **All the sick** *were* hospitalized.
- **The old** *are* greatly respected.
- **The unemployed** *are* losing hope.
- **The beauty** *are* always charming.

88. **Study, how verbs change its forms according to Tense** and Nouns as its subjects in the sentence:

Tense	Types	Function/Definition	Examples
Present Tense	Indefinite	Habit and general action	I write. He writes
	Continuous	Action going on	I am writing. He is writing.
	Perfect	Just completed action (whose time is not given)	I have written. He has written.
	Perfect Continuous	Started in the past and still going on	I have been writing. He has been writing.

Tense	Types	Function/Definition	Examples
Past Tense	Indefinite	Action completed in the past	I wrote. He wrote.
	Continuous	Action continuing in the past	I was writing. He was writing.
	Perfect	Action done earlier than another action in past	I had written. He had written.
	Perfect Continuous	Action continued for some time in the past	I had been writing. He had been writing.

Tense	Types	Function/ Definition	Examples
Future Tense	Indefinite	Action to happen in the future	I shall write. He will write.
	Continuous	Action to continue in the future	I shall be writing. He will be writing
	Perfect	Action will be complete before a particular time in the future	I shall have written. He will have written.
	Perfect Continuous	Action to continue for some time in the future and also end in the future.	I shall have been writing. He will have been writing.

89. Sequence of Tense:

Sequence of tense occurs in sentences with clauses in Narration Change. It tells about the rules that the tense in the main clause should govern the tense in the sub-clauses.

- 1) If the main clause is in the present or future tense the verb in the sub-clause may be in any tense.
- But if the main clause is in the past tense, the verb in the sub-clause must be in the past tense.

Study the examples of Sequence of Tense in the following chart:

Main clause	Sub-clause
He says /will say	that he went to school. (Past Tense) that he goes to school. (Present Tense) that he will go to school. (Future Tense)
He said	that he was ill. that he had gone. that he was going. /that he went.
Note:	For details, please study the chapter of Narration Change

About Mr. Peter

Mr. Peter is a penname of the writer, an Indian and a teacher in West Bengal. Most of his academic works are the products of his professional career what he held over twenty years and continuing… Mr. Peter loves to publish his books in the self-publishing platforms, like Amazon (worldwide) and notionpress.com (India). For this, Peter heartily pays his gratitude to Amazon, notionpress.com and for marketing to Flipkart, Amazon & different social media. Presently, Mr. Peter's books are available in 3 formats—eBook, Paperback & Hardcover. Mr. Peter's books which are published at Notion Press Pvt. Ltd., Chennai, are available to buy on **notionpress.com, Flipkart**, **Amazon**.in

Discounts, promotions, etc. are available in all platforms. However, if one seeks special offers for marketing or wants to give bulk order, s/he may visit only to **notionpress.com** (type **Mr. Peter** in the search box, and use following **Coupon Codes:** (If not work, for the current status, one may contact by https://www.facebook.com/profile.php?id=100081822070172 or (5) Books Campaigns, Free Coupons, Learning English Grammar & Composition | Facebook

notionpress.com/en/coupon_manager

books Author Dashboard My Shelf

Campaign Name	Book Name	Coupon Type	Discount %	Discounted Price	Used Count	Report	Actions
	Peter's 'English Grammar'	Bulk-Use	30	₹ 841	0/100		
	Peter's 'English Grammar'	Multi-Use	23	₹ 925	0/100		
	A Book of Advanced Writing Skill, the Complete Version (incl Part 1, 2 & 3)	Bulk-Use	23	₹ 601	1/100		
	A Book of Advanced Writing Skill, the Complete Version (incl Part-1, 2 & 3)	Multi-Use	15	₹ 663	0/100		
	Development of Writing Skill, Part-3	Bulk Use	24	₹ 278	0/10		
	Development of Writing Skill, Part-3	Multi-Use	18	₹ 300	0/10		
	Development of Writing Skill, Part-2	Bulk-Use	24	₹ 278	1/10		
	Development of Writing Skill, Part-2	Multi-Use	18	₹ 300	0/10		
	Steps to Composition (Development of Writing Skill, from Primary to Secondary Level)	Multi-Use	20	₹ 240	1/10		
	Rhetoric & Prosody	Multi-Use	20	₹ 192	0/10		
	Question Bank of English Grammar & Composition	Multi-Use	20	₹ 448	0/10		
	Study of Subject-Verb Agreement, Narration Change, Use of Punctuation; including Analysis, Synthesis & Split-up	Multi-Use	20	₹ 241	0/10		
	Detail Study of Phrases, Clauses & Sentences, including Idioms & Phrasal Verbs	Multi-Use	20	₹ 232	0/10		
	Study of Adverbs, Prepositions, Conjunctions & Interjections	Multi-Use	20	₹ 208	0/10		

www.ingramcontent.com/pod-product-compliance
Ingram Content Group UK Ltd.
Pitfield, Milton Keynes, MK11 3LW, UK
UKHW021915190726
13853UKWH00002B/678

9 798887 046747